# The Person of the Holy Spirit

# THE PERSON OF THE HOLY SPIRIT

R. D. ELDERS

PALMETTO
PUBLISHING

Charleston, SC
www.PalmettoPublishing.com

***The Person of the Holy Spirit***



First Edition

Paperback ISBN: 978-1-64990-945-9
eBook ISBN: 978-1-64990-676-2

# TABLE OF CONTENTS

# INTRODUCTION

## INTRO:

**Many times the Holy Spirit is looked upon as the power of God working the miraculous in individual lives. It is true that the Holy Spirit is power. Acts 1:8** ***But ye shall receive power, after that the Holy Ghost is come upon you: and ye shall be witnesses unto me both in Jerusalem, and in all Judaea, and in Samaria, and unto the uttermost part of the earth.*** **The Holy Spirit is more than just power or an influence to be used. The Holy Spirit is a person of the Godhead. If He is a person, it then places one in a different relationship with Him. A relationship with a person requires a "working together", rather than using a force at your own will. If you are working with God you are the one expected to take instruction with obedience to follow.**

**1.** The Holy Spirit is given to us that He may abide, dwell, or live in us as His temple.
John 14:16-17 KJV

*16 And I will pray the Father, and he shall give you another Comforter, that he may abide with you forever;*
*17 Even the Spirit of truth; whom the world cannot receive, because it seeth him not, neither knoweth him: but ye know him; for he dwelleth with you, and shall be in you.*

**a.** He will dwell with you, or stay in a given place, relation or expectancy.

**b.** He shall be in you, denoting a fixed position in place, time, or state. It is a position of rest and continuance.

**1 Cor. 3:16** *Know ye not that ye are the temple of God, and that the Spirit of God dwelleth in you? KJV*

**2.** If one looks upon the Holy Spirit to be a force you miss fellowship with the Spirit.
Phil 2:1 KJV

*1 If there be therefore any consolation in Christ, if any comfort of love, if any fellowship of the Spirit, if any bowels and mercies,*

**a.** Fellowship is the Greek word "koinonia," which means partnership, participation, a sharer. It comes from the Greek root word "sun" which is a preposition denoting union.

3. The very name of God means one to be worshipped. Your ability to worship is hindered if you think of Him as an impersonal influence or power. We are robbing a divine person of the worship and love which is His due.

   **Ex. 34:14** *For thou shalt worship no other god: for the LORD, whose name is Jealous, is a jealous God: KJV*

   **1 Chron. 16:29** *Give unto the LORD the glory due unto his name: bring an offering, and come before him: worship the LORD in the beauty of holiness. KJV*

   a. Worship means to depress, i.e. prostrate (especially reflexive, in homage to royalty or God):

      **Matt. 2:2** *Saying, Where is he that is born King of the Jews? for we have seen his star in the east, and are come to worship him. KJV*

   b. Worship in the New Testament means to kiss, like a dog licking his master's hand, to fawn or crouch to, i.e. (literally or figuratively) prostrate oneself in homage (do reverence to, adore):

      **John 4:23-24 KJV**
      *23 But the hour cometh, and now is, when the true worshippers shall worship the Father in spirit and in truth: for the Father seeketh such to worship him.*
      *24 God is a Spirit: and they that worship him must worship him in spirit and in truth.*

4. It is important from the practical standpoint

   a. If He is just an influence or power, we will say, "How can I get hold of the Holy Spirit and use it?

   b. If we think of the Holy Spirit as a divine person our attitude will be, "How does the Holy Spirit use me? This brings an attitude of humility rather than pride.

5. It is important from the standpoint of experience – it becomes a working relationship between yourself and the Holy Spirit

   a. You have a person of the Godhead indwelling you. 1 Cor. 3:16-17 KJV

      *16 Know ye not that ye are the temple of God, and that the Spirit of God dwelleth in you?*
      *17 If any man defile the temple of God, him shall God destroy; for the temple of God is holy, which temple ye are.*

      **2 Cor. 13:14** *The grace of the Lord Jesus Christ, and the love of God, and the communion of the Holy Ghost, be with you all. Amen. (KJV)*

      **Rom. 8:14-17 KJV**
      *14 For as many as are led by the Spirit of God, they are the sons of God.*
      *15 For ye have not received the spirit of bondage again to fear; but ye have received the Spirit of adoption, whereby we cry, Abba, Father.*

*16 The Spirit itself beareth witness with our spirit, that we are the children of God:*
*17 And if children, then heirs; heirs of God, and joint-heirs with Christ; if so be that we suffer with him, that we may be also glorified together.*

**1 Cor. 3:9** *For we are laborers together with God: ye are God's husbandry, ye are God's building. KJV*

**2 Cor. 6:1** *We then, as workers together with him, beseech you also that ye receive not the grace of God in vain. KJV*

6. The Lord Jesus used personal pronouns in speaking about the Holy Spirit. Even Jesus taught respect concerning the Spirit. Note the pronouns used in the words of Jesus. They are all in the masculine gender. The word "Spirit" is in the neuter gender, which is neither masculine nor feminine in gender. According to Greek usage, the pronouns that refer to the Spirit should also be neuter.

**John 14:16-17 KJV**

*16 And I will pray the Father, and he shall give you another Comforter, that **he** may abide with you forever;*
*17 Even the Spirit of truth; whom the world cannot receive, because it seeth him not, neither knoweth **him**: but ye know him; for **he** dwelleth with you, and shall be in you.*

**John 14:26** *But the Comforter, which is the Holy Ghost, whom the Father will send in my name, **he** shall teach you all things, and bring all things to your remembrance, whatsoever I have said unto you. KJV*

**John 15:26** *But when the Comforter is come, whom I will send unto you from the Father, even the Spirit of truth, which proceedeth from the Father, **he** shall testify of me: KJV*

**John 16:7-8 KJV**

*7 Nevertheless I tell you the truth; It is expedient for you that I go away: for if I go not away, the Comforter will not come unto you; but if I depart, I will send **him** unto you.*
*8 And when **he** is come, **he** will reprove the world of sin, and of righteousness, and of judgment:*

**John 16:13-14 KJV**

*13 Howbeit when **he**, the Spirit of truth, is come, **he** will guide you into all truth: for **he** shall not speak of **himself**; but whatsoever **he** shall hear, that shall **he** speak: and **he** will shew you things to come.*
*14 **He** shall glorify me: for **he** shall receive of mine, and shall shew it unto you.*

**I. The subject of the Holy Spirit is really a study of the third person of the Trinity. The Bible has much to say concerning the person, work, and the gifts that are distributed by Him. We will define the very word "Holy Spirit".**

**A. Old Testament – Law of First Mention**

**Gen. 1:2** *And the earth was without form, and void; and darkness was upon the face of the deep. And the Spirit of God moved upon the face of the waters. KJV*

**Ps. 51:11** *Cast me not away from thy presence; and take not thy Holy Spirit from me. KJV*

1. **Holy** SC OT: a sacred place or thing; rarely abstract, sanctity:

   a. SC OT: a primitive root; to be (causatively, make, pronounce or observe as) clean (ceremonially or morally):

2. **Spirit** SC OT: wind; by resemblance breath, i.e. a sensible (or even violent) exhalation; figuratively, life, anger, unsubstantiality; by extension, a region of the sky; by resemblance spirit, but only of a rational being (including its expression and functions):

   a. SC OT: a primitive root; properly, to blow, i.e. breathe; only (literally) to smell or (by implication, perceive (figuratively, to anticipate)

**B. New Testament – Holy Spirit**

**Matt. 1:18** *Now the birth of Jesus Christ was on this wise: When as his mother Mary was espoused to Joseph, before they came together, she was found with child of the Holy Ghost. KJV*

**Matt. 3:16** *And Jesus, when he was baptized, went up straightway out of the water: and, lo, the heavens were opened unto him, and he saw the Spirit of God descending like a dove, and lighting upon him: KJV*

1. **Holy** SC NT: sacred (physically, pure, morally blameless or religious, ceremonially, consecrated)

   a. SC NT: properly, clean, i.e. (figuratively) innocent, modest, perfect

   b. SC NT: to warm; to brood, i.e. (figuratively) to foster

2. **Spirit** SC NT: a current of air, i.e. breath (blast) or a breeze; by analogy or figuratively, a spirit, i.e. (human) the rational soul, (by implication) vital principle, mental disposition, etc., or (superhuman) an angel, demon, or (divine) God, Christ's spirit, the Holy Spirit

   a. SC NT: a primary word; to breathe hard, i.e. breeze

3. The word Spirit in the New Testament breaks down the four realms of the spirit world.

   a. The human spirit 1 Thess. 5:23 KJV

      *23 And the very God of peace sanctify you wholly; and I pray God your whole spirit and soul and body be preserved blameless unto the coming of our Lord Jesus Christ.*

   b. The angels as spirits - The divine Heb. 1:13-14 KJV

      *13 But to which of the angels said he at any time, Sit on my right hand, until I make thine enemies thy footstool?*
      *14 Are they not all ministering spirits, sent forth to minister for them who shall be heirs of salvation?*

**c.** The evil spirits – demons, Devil Mark 1:26 KJV

*26 And when the unclean spirit had torn him, and cried with a loud voice, he came out of him.*

Acts 19:14-15 KJV
*14 And there were seven sons of one Sceva, a Jew, and chief of the priests, which did so.*
*15 And the evil spirit answered and said, Jesus I know, and Paul I know; but who are ye?*

**d.** The Holy Spirit Luke 3:21-22 KJV

*21 Now when all the people were baptized, it came to pass, that Jesus also being baptized, and praying, the heaven was opened,*
*22 And the Holy Ghost descended in a bodily shape like a dove upon him, and a voice came from heaven, which said, Thou art my beloved Son; in thee I am well pleased.*

**4.** The words Holy Spirit and Holy Ghost are one in the same. They both have the same meaning.

## II. Other scriptures help us to understand the meaning of the Holy Spirit.

### A. Jesus breathed upon his disciples and said receive the Holy Spirit. John 20:21-22 KJV

*21 Then said Jesus to them again, Peace be unto you: as my Father hath sent me, even so send I you.*
*22 And when he had said this, he breathed on them, and saith unto them, Receive ye the Holy Ghost:*

**1. Breathed** SC NT: (to puff) to blow at or on

### B. When God created man He breathed into him the breath of life. Job 33:4 KJV

*4 The Spirit of God hath made me, and the breath of the Almighty hath given me life.*

**1. Spirit** SC OT: wind; by resemblance breath, i.e. a sensible (or even violent) exhalation; figuratively, life, anger, unsubstantiality; by extension, a region of the sky; by resemblance spirit, but only of a rational being (including its expression and functions):

**Gen. 2:7** *And the LORD God formed man of the dust of the ground, and breathed into his nostrils the breath of life; and man became a living soul. KJV*

### C. The Holy Spirit gave life to the dry bones in Ezekiel 37:7-10 KJV

*7 So I prophesied as I was commanded: and as I prophesied, there was a noise, and behold a shaking, and the bones came together, bone to his bone.*
*8 And when I beheld, lo, the sinews and the flesh came up upon them, and the skin covered them above: but there was no breath in them.*

*9 Then said he unto me, Prophesy unto the wind, prophesy, son of man, and say to the wind, Thus saith the Lord GOD; Come from the four winds, O breath, and breathe upon these slain, that they may live.*
*10 So I prophesied as he commanded me, and the breath came into them, and they lived, and stood up upon their feet, an exceeding great army.*

# THE SPIRIT OF MAN

## INTRO:

**In defining the word "Spirit" there are four different categories revealed. Each category is a study within itself. For the purpose of this chapter, we will only deal with the spirit of man.**

1. Man's spirit
2. Angelic beings – angels or spirits
3. Satan and demonic spirits
4. The Holy Spirit

**I. This chapter will consider the spirit of man**

**A. Man is a tri-part being – SPIRIT SOUL AND BODY I Thess. 5:23 KJV**

*23 And the very God of peace sanctify you wholly; and I pray God your whole spirit and soul and body be preserved blameless unto the coming of our Lord Jesus Christ.*

**Job 32:8** *But there is a spirit in man: and the inspiration of the Almighty giveth them understanding. KJV*

**B. The LORD forms man's spirit within him Zech. 12:1 KJV**

*1 The burden of the word of the LORD for Israel, saith the LORD, which stretcheth forth the heavens, and layeth the foundation of the earth, and formeth the spirit of man within him.*

1. **Formeth** SC OT: (through the squeezing into shape); to mold into a form; especially as a potter; figuratively, to determine (i.e. form a resolution)
2. SC OT: to press (intransitive), i.e. be narrow; figuratively, be in distress

**C. God speaks and deals with man in his spirit. Prov. 20:27 KJV**

*27 The spirit of man is the candle of the LORD, searching all the inward parts of the belly.*

**Prov. 20:27** *The spirit of a man is the lamp of the LORD, Searching all the inner depths of his heart. NKJV*

**Prov. 20:27** *A man's conscience is the Lord's searchlight exposing his hidden motives. TLB*

**Prov. 20:27** *The LORD's searchlight penetrates the human spirit, NLT*

**Prov. 20:27** *The spirit of man [that factor in human personality which proceeds immediately from God] is the lamp of the Lord, searching all his innermost parts. [1 Cor. 2:11] AMP*

**D. When a person dies his spirit returns to God. Eccl. 3:20-21 KJV**

*20 All go unto one place; all are of the dust, and all turn to dust again.*
*21 Who knoweth the spirit of man that goeth upward, and the spirit of the beast that goeth downward to the earth?*

**1 Thess. 4:15-17 AMP**
*15 For this we declare to you by the Lord's [own] word, that we who are alive and remain until the coming of the Lord shall in no way precede [into His presence] or have any advantage at all over those who have previously fallen asleep [in Him in death].*
*16 For the Lord Himself will descend from heaven with a loud cry of summons, with the shout of an archangel, and with the blast of the trumpet of God. And those who have departed this life in Christ will rise first.*
*17 Then we, the living ones who remain [on the earth], shall simultaneously be caught up along with [the resurrected dead] in the clouds to meet the Lord in the air; and so always (through the eternity of the eternities) we shall be with the Lord!*

**Eccl. 8:8** *There is no man that hath power over the spirit to retain the spirit; neither hath he power in the day of death: and there is no discharge in that war; neither shall wickedness deliver those that are given to it. KJV*

**Eccl. 12:7** *Then shall the dust return to the earth as it was: and the spirit shall return unto God who gave it. KJV*

**Jam. 2:26** *For as the body without the spirit is dead, so faith without works is dead also. KJV*

1. Jesus committed His spirit to God at the time of His death

   **Ps. 31:5** *Into thine hand I commit my spirit: thou hast redeemed me, O LORD God of truth. KJV*

   **Matt. 27:50** *Jesus, when he had cried again with a loud voice, yielded up the ghost. KJV*

   **Matt. 27:50** *And Jesus cried again with a loud voice and gave up His spirit. AMP*

2. Man does not understand how the spirit of man is formed in the womb Eccl. 11:5 KJV

*5 As thou knowest not what is the way of the spirit, nor how the bones do grow in the womb of her that is with child: even so thou knowest not the works of God who maketh all.*

**E. The Lord is called the "God of the spirits of all men". He is Spirit and Lord overall Spirits Num. 16:20-22 KJV**

*20 And the LORD spake unto Moses and unto Aaron, saying,*
*21 Separate yourselves from among this congregation, that I may consume them in a moment.*
*22 And they fell upon their faces, and said, O God, the God of the spirits of all flesh, shall one man sin, and wilt thou be wroth with all the congregation?*

**Num. 27:15-16 KJV**
*15 And Moses spake unto the LORD, saying,*
*16 Let the LORD, the God of the spirits of all flesh, set a man over the congregation,*

**II. The scriptures talk much about the spirit of man**

**A. He can be troubled in his spirit Gen. 41:8 KJV**

*8 And it came to pass in the morning that his spirit was troubled; and he sent and called for all the magicians of Egypt, and all the wise men thereof: and Pharaoh told them his dream; but there was none that could interpret them unto Pharaoh.*

1. **Troubled** SC OT: to tap, i.e. beat regularly; hence (generally) to impel or agitate

**Job 21:4** *As for me, is my complaint to man? And if it were so, why should not my spirit be troubled? KJV*

**Dan. 2:1-3 KJV**
*1 And in the second year of the reign of Nebuchadnezzar, Nebuchadnezzar dreamed dreams, wherewith his spirit was troubled, and his sleep brake from him.*
*3 And the king said unto them, I have dreamed a dream, and my spirit was troubled to know the dream.*

**B. When encouragement is given reviving can come to the spirit of man Gen. 45:27-28 KJV**

*27 And they told him all the words of Joseph, which he had said unto them: and when he saw the wagons which Joseph had sent to carry him, the spirit of Jacob their father revived:*
*28 And Israel said, It is enough; Joseph my son is yet alive: I will go and see him before I die.*

1. **Revived** SC OT: to live, whether literally or figuratively; causatively, to revive

**C. A man can become impatient in spirit Ex. 6:9 KJV**

*9 And Moses spake so unto the children of Israel: but they hearkened not unto Moses for anguish of spirit, and for cruel bondage.*

1. **Anguish** SC OT: shortness (of spirit), i.e. impatience

    a. SC OT: to dock off, i.e. curtail (transitive or intransitive, literal or figurative); especially to harvest (grass or grain):

**D. Man's spirit can be hardened Deut. 2:30 KJV**

*30 But Sihon king of Heshbon would not let us pass by him: for the LORD thy God hardened his spirit, and made his heart obstinate, that he might deliver him into thy hand, as appeareth this day.*

1. **Hardened** SC OT: to be dense, i.e. tough or severe (in various applications)

**E. When a person is without spirit they are conquered. Joshua 5:1 KJV**

*1 And it came to pass, when all the kings of the Amorites, which were on the side of Jordan westward, and all the kings of the Canaanites, which were by the sea, heard that the LORD had dried up the waters of Jordan from before the children of Israel, until we were passed over, that their heart melted, neither was there spirit in them anymore, because of the children of Israel.*

**F. Difficult circumstances in life can cause one to have a sorrowful spirit I Sam. 1:15 KJV**

*15 And Hannah answered and said, No, my lord, I am a woman of a sorrowful spirit: I have drunk neither wine nor strong drink, but have poured out my soul before the LORD.*

**G. In the natural food can revive the sick. Likewise for the spiritual man a word can revive the sick in spirit I Sam. 30:11-13 KJV**

*11 And they found an Egyptian in the field, and brought him to David, and gave him bread, and he did eat; and they made him drink water;*
*12 And they gave him a piece of a cake of figs, and two clusters of raisins: and when he had eaten, his spirit came again to him: for he had eaten no bread, nor drunk any water, three days and three nights.*
*13 And David said unto him, To whom belongest thou? and whence art thou? And he said, I am a young man of Egypt, servant to an Amalekite; and my master left me, because three days agone I fell sick.*

**Ps. 119:154** *Plead my cause, and deliver me: quicken me according to thy word. KJV*

**H. The awesomeness of God's work moves one to a condition of wonderment – note queen Sheba's response 1 Kings 10:4-5 KJV**

*4 And when the queen of Sheba had seen all Solomon's wisdom, and the house that he had built,*
*5 And the meat of his table, and the sitting of his servants, and the attendance of his ministers, and their apparel, and his cupbearers, and his ascent by which he went up unto the house of the LORD; there was no more spirit in her.*

**I. God can use mankind to fulfill His word by stirring up his spirit.**

**1.** Pul king of Assyria I Chron. 5:26 KJV

*26 And the God of Israel stirred up the spirit of Pul king of Assyria, and the spirit of Tilgath-pilneser king of Assyria, and he carried them away, even the Reubenites, and the Gadites, and the half tribe of Manasseh, and brought them unto Halah, and Habor, and Hara, and to the river Gozan, unto this day.*

**2.** The Philistines 2 Chron. 21:16 KJV

*16 Moreover the LORD stirred up against Jehoram the spirit of the Philistines, and of the Arabians, that were near the Ethiopians:*

**3.** Cyrus king of Persia 2 Chron. 36:22 KJV

*22 Now in the first year of Cyrus king of Persia, that the word of the LORD spoken by the mouth of Jeremiah might be accomplished, the LORD stirred up the spirit of Cyrus king of Persia, that he made a proclamation throughout all his kingdom, and put it also in writing, saying,*

**Ezra 1:1** *Now in the first year of Cyrus king of Persia, that the word of the LORD by the mouth of Jeremiah might be fulfilled, the LORD stirred up the spirit of Cyrus king of Persia, that he made a proclamation throughout all his kingdom, and put it also in writing, saying, KJV*

**4.** The spirit of Zerubbabel Hag. 1:14 KJV

*14 And the LORD stirred up the spirit of Zerubbabel the son of Shealtiel, governor of Judah, and the spirit of Joshua the son of Josedech, the high priest, and the spirit of all the remnant of the people; and they came and did work in the house of the LORD of hosts, their God,*

**J. God will stir up man's spirit with vision Ezra 1:5 KJV**

*5 Then rose up the chief of the fathers of Judah and Benjamin, and the priests, and the Levites, with all them whose spirit God had raised, to go up to build the house of the LORD which is in Jerusalem.*

**K. Man can absorb wrong things into his spirit Job 6:4 KJV**

*4 For the arrows of the Almighty are within me, the poison whereof drinketh up my spirit: the terrors of God do set themselves in array against me.*

**1. Drinketh** – imbibe to absorb or take in as if by drinking. To receive and absorb into the mind

**L. Pressure can bring a crowding or a narrow place to one's spirit Job 7:11 KJV**

*11 Therefore I will not refrain my mouth; I will speak in the anguish of my spirit; I will complain in the bitterness of my soul.*

1. **Anguish** SC OT: narrow; (as a noun) a tight place (usually figuratively, i.e. trouble); also a pebble (as in OT: 6864); (transitive) an opponent (as crowding)

   a. SC OT: to cramp, literally or figuratively

**M. The visitation of God preserves man's spirit Job 10:12 KJV**

*12 Thou hast granted me life and favor, and thy visitation hath preserved my spirit.*

1. **Visitation** SC OT: visitation (in many senses, chiefly official)

   a. SC OT: to visit (with friendly or hostile intent); by analogy, to oversee, muster, charge, care for, miss, deposit, etc.

2. **Preserved** SC OT properly, to hedge about (as with thorns), i.e. guard; generally, to protect, attend to, etc.

**N. We have answers within – even in our own spirit Job 20:3 KJV**

*3 I have heard the check of my reproach, and the spirit of my understanding causeth me to answer.*

**Job 20:3** *I have heard the reproof which puts me to shame, but out of my understanding, my spirit answers me. AMP*

**O. Our spirit is to be clean. Ps. 32:2 KJV**

*2 Blessed is the man unto whom the LORD imputeth not iniquity, and in whose spirit there is no guile.*

1. **Guile** SC OT: remissness, treachery

   a. SC OT: to hurl; specifically, to shoot; figuratively, to delude or betray (as if causing to fall)

**P. We are to have a contrite spirit. Ps. 34:18 KJV**

*18 The LORD is nigh unto them that are of a broken heart; and saveth such as be of a contrite spirit.*

1. **Contrite** SC OT: crushed (literally powder, or figuratively, contrite)

   a. SC OT: to crumble; transitively, to bruise (literally or figuratively)

   b. SC OT: to collapse (phys. or mentally):

**Q. King David repents from his sin and asks for two things, create in me a clean heart and renew a right spirit within me Ps. 51:10 KJV**

*10 Create in me a clean heart, O God; and renew a right spirit within me.*

1. **Renew** SC OT: to be new; causatively, to rebuild

2. **Right** SC OT: properly, to be erect (i.e. stand perpendicular); hence (causatively) to set up, in a great variety of applications, whether literal (establish, fix, prepare, apply), or figurative (appoint, render sure, proper or prosperous)

**R. God accepts the sacrifice of a broken spirit. Ps. 51:17 KJV**

*17 The sacrifices of God are a broken spirit: a broken and a contrite heart, O God, thou wilt not despise.*

1. **Broken** SC OT: to burst (literally or figuratively)

**S. Man can become overwhelmed in his spirit. Ps. 77:3 KJV**

*3 I remembered God, and was troubled: I complained, and my spirit was overwhelmed. Selah.*

1. **Overwhelmed** SC OT: to shroud, i.e. clothe (whether transitive or reflex.); hence (from the idea of darkness) to languish

**Ps. 142:3-4 KJV**

*3 When my spirit was overwhelmed within me, then thou knewest my path. In the way wherein I walked have they privily laid a snare for me.*
*4 Therefore is my spirit overwhelmed within me; my heart within me is desolate.*

**T. We search out God in our spirit Ps. 77:6 KJV**

*6 I call to remembrance my song in the night: I commune with mine own heart: and my spirit made diligent search.*

**U. Our resolve must come from our spirit Ps. 78:8 KJV**

*8 And might not be as their fathers, a stubborn and rebellious generation; a generation that set not their heart aright, and whose spirit was not steadfast with God.*

**V. Our spirit has the capacity to come to an end Ps. 143:7 KJV**

*7 Hear me speedily, O LORD: my spirit faileth: hide not thy face from me, lest I be like unto them that go down into the pit.*

1. **Faileth** SC OT: to end, whether intransitive (to cease, be finished, perish) or transitively (to complete, prepare, consume)

W. **Our spirit is to be one of support, permanent, or quiet Prov. 11:13 KJV**

*13 A talebearer revealeth secrets: but he that is of a faithful spirit concealeth the matter.*

1. **Faithful** SC OT: properly, to build up or support; to foster as a parent or nurse; figuratively to render (or be) firm or faithful, to trust or believe, to be permanent or quiet; morally to be true or certain

X. **We can be hasty in spirit Prov. 14:29 KJV**

*29 He that is slow to wrath is of great understanding: but he that is hasty of spirit exalteth folly.*

1. **Hasty** SC OT: short (whether in size, number, life, strength or temper)

2. SC OT: to dock off, i.e. curtail (transitive or intransitive, literal or figurative); especially to harvest (grass or grain)

Y. **The tongue with its power of death and life can break down the spirit Prov. 15:4 KJV**

*4 A wholesome tongue is a tree of life: but perverseness therein is a breach in the spirit.*

1. **Perverseness** SC OT: distortion, i.e. (figuratively) viciousness

   a. SC OT: properly, to wrench, i.e. (figuratively) to subvert

2. **Breach** SC OT: a fracture, figuratively, ruin; specifically, a solution (of a dream)

   a. SC OT: to burst (literally or figuratively)

**Prov. 15:4** *A gentle tongue [with its healing power] is a tree of life, but willful contrariness in it breaks down the spirit. AMP*

Z. **Man's spirit can be broken Prov. 15:13 KJV**

*13 A merry heart maketh a cheerful countenance: but by sorrow of the heart the spirit is broken.*

1. **Sorrow** SC OT: an idol; also, a pain or wound

2. **Broken** SC OT: smitten, i.e. (figuratively) afflicted

   a. SC OT: to smite, i.e. drive away

**Prov. 17:22** *A merry heart doeth good like a medicine: but a broken spirit drieth the bones. KJV*

**Prov. 18:14** *The spirit of a man will sustain his infirmity; but a wounded spirit who can bear? KJV*

## III. Continuing with the spirit of man

### A. A man can become proud in his spirit Prov. 16:18 KJV

*18 Pride goeth before destruction, and a haughty spirit before a fall.*

1. **Haughty** SC OT: elation, grandeur, arrogance

    a. SC OT: 1361 to soar, i.e. be lofty; figuratively, to be haughty

**Prov. 16:19** *Better it is to be of an humble spirit with the lowly, than to divide the spoil with the proud. KJV*

**Prov. 29:23** *A man's pride shall bring him low: but honour shall uphold the humble in spirit. KJV*

**Eccl. 7:8** *Better is the end of a thing than the beginning thereof: and the patient in spirit is better than the proud in spirit. KJV*

### B. We are to rule our spirit Prov. 16:32 KJV

*32 He that is slow to anger is better than the mighty, and he that ruleth his spirit than he that taketh a city.*

1. **Rule** SC OT: to rule

**Prov. 25:28** *He that hath no rule over his own spirit is like a city that is broken down, and without walls. KJV*

### C. We are to have an excellent spirit Prov. 17:27 KJV

*27 He that hath knowledge spareth his words: and a man of understanding is of an excellent spirit.*

1. **Excellent** SC OT: from an unused root meaning to chill; cool; figuratively, quiet

**Dan. 5:12** *Forasmuch as an excellent spirit, and knowledge, and understanding, interpreting of dreams, and shewing of hard sentences, and dissolving of doubts, were found in the same Daniel, whom the king named Belteshazzar: now let Daniel be called, and he will shew the interpretation. KJV*

**Dan. 6:3** *Then this Daniel was preferred above the presidents and princes, because an excellent spirit was in him; and the king thought to set him over the whole realm. KJV*

1. **Excellent** SC OT: preeminent; as an adverb, very

**D. We are to have a humble spirit Isa. 57:15 KJV**

*15 For thus saith the high and lofty One that inhabiteth eternity, whose name is Holy; I dwell in the high and holy place, with him also that is of a contrite and humble spirit, to revive the spirit of the humble, and to revive the heart of the contrite ones.*

**E. Works for work's sake is an emptiness of spirit Eccl. 1:14 KJV**

*14 I have seen all the works that are done under the sun; and, behold, all is vanity and vexation of spirit.*

**Eccl. 1:14** *I have seen all the works that are done under the sun, and behold, all is vanity, a striving after the wind and a feeding on wind. AMP*

**F. We can be grieved in spirit Isa. 54:6 KJV**

*6 For the LORD hath called thee as a woman forsaken and grieved in spirit, and a wife of youth, when thou wast refused, saith thy God.*

1. **Grieved** SC OT: properly, to carve, i.e. fabricate or fashion; hence (in a bad sense) to worry, pain or anger

**Dan. 7:15** *I Daniel was grieved in my spirit in the midst of my body, and the visions of my head troubled me. KJV*

**G. Our spirit can faint Ezek. 21:7 KJV**

*7 And it shall be, when they say unto thee, Wherefore sighest thou? that thou shalt answer, For the tidings; because it cometh: and every heart shall melt, and all hands shall be feeble, and every spirit shall faint, and all knees shall be weak as water: behold, it cometh, and shall be brought to pass, saith the Lord GOD.*

1. **Faint** SC OT: to be weak, i.e. (figuratively) to despond (causatively, rebuke), or (of light, the eye) to grow dull

## V. Continuation of man's spirit in the New Testament - Paul teaches much about our spirit.

**A. We are to serve the Son with our spirit Rom. 1:9 KJV**

*9 For God is my witness, whom I serve with my spirit in the gospel of his Son, that without ceasing I make mention of you always in my prayers;*

1. **Serve** SC NT: (a hired menial); to minister (to God), i.e. render, religious homage

**B. Our spirit is to bear witness with the Holy Spirit. Rom. 8:16 KJV**

*16 The Spirit itself beareth witness with our spirit, that we are the children of God:*

1. **Witness** SC NT: to testify jointly, i.e. corroborate by (concurrent) evidence

C. **Fervency of spirit is an attitude that every believer must have. Rom. 12:11 KJV**

*11 Not slothful in business; fervent in spirit; serving the Lord;*

1. **Fervent** SC NT: verb; to be hot (boil, of liquids; or glow, of solids), i.e. (figuratively) be fervid (earnest)

D. **By and through our spirit, we are to know God's thoughts 1 Cor. 2:11 KJV**

*11 For what man knoweth the things of a man, save the spirit of man which is in him? even so the things of God knoweth no man, but the Spirit of God.*

**1 Cor. 2:11** *For what person perceives (knows and understands) what passes through a man's thoughts except the man's own spirit within him? Just so no one discerns (comes to know and comprehend) the thoughts of God except the Spirit of God. AMP*

E. **We are to glorify God in our spirit. I Cor. 6:20 KJV**

*20 For ye are bought with a price: therefore glorify God in your body, and in your spirit, which are God's.*

1. **Glorify** SC NT: to render (or esteem) glorious (in a wide application)

   a. SC NT: glory (as very apparent), in a wide application (literal or figurative, objective or subjective)

**Phil. 3:3** *For we are the circumcision, which worship God in the spirit, and rejoice in Christ Jesus, and have no confidence in the flesh. KJV*

F. **We are to pray with our spirit. I Cor. 14:14-16 KJV**

*14 For if I pray in an unknown tongue, my spirit prayeth, but my understanding is unfruitful.*
*15 What is it then? I will pray with the spirit, and I will pray with the understanding also: I will sing with the spirit, and I will sing with the understanding also.*
*16 Else when thou shalt bless with the spirit, how shall he that occupieth the room of the unlearned say Amen at thy giving of thanks, seeing he understandeth not what thou sayest?*

G. **We can refresh one another in spirit I Cor. 16:18 KJV**

*18 For they have refreshed my spirit and yours: therefore acknowledge ye them that are such.*

1. **Refreshed** SC NT: (reflexively) to repose (literally or figuratively [be exempt], remain); by implication, to refresh

**H. The woman is to have a meek and quiet spirit. 1 Pet. 3:1-4 AMP**

*1 IN LIKE manner, you married women, be submissive to your own husbands [subordinate yourselves as being secondary to and dependent on them, and adapt yourselves to them], so that even if any do not obey the Word [of God], they may be won over not by discussion but by the [godly] lives of their wives,*
*2 When they observe the pure and modest way in which you conduct yourselves, together with your reverence [for your husband; you are to feel for him all that reverence includes: to respect, defer to, revere him--to honor, esteem, appreciate, prize, and, in the human sense, to adore him, that is, to admire, praise, be devoted to, deeply love, and enjoy your husband].*
*3 Let not yours be the [merely] external adorning with [elaborate] interweaving and knotting of the hair, the wearing of jewelry, or changes of clothes;*
*4 But let it be the inward adorning and beauty of the hidden person of the heart, with the incorruptible and unfading charm of a gentle and peaceful spirit, which [is not anxious or wrought up, but] is very precious in the sight of God.*

1. **Meek** SC NT: apparently a primary word; mild, i.e. (by implication) humble

2. **Quiet** SC NT: properly, keeping one's seat (sedentary), i.e. (by implication) still (undisturbed, undisturbing)

**I. The word of God divides asunder the soul and spirit. Heb. 4:12 KJV**

*12 For the word of God is quick, and powerful, and sharper than any two-edged sword, piercing even to the dividing asunder of soul and spirit, and of the joints and marrow, and is a discerner of the thoughts and intents of the heart. KJV*

1. **Dividing Asunder** SC NT: a separation or distribution

**J. Paul exhorts Timothy to be an example of the believers in spirit. I Tim. 4:12 KJV**

*12 Let no man despise thy youth; but be thou an example of the believers, in word, in conversation, in charity, in spirit, in faith, in purity.*

**K. Our spirit can be in turmoil – that is without rest concerning unsettling circumstances 2 Cor. 2:13 KJV**

*13 I had no rest in my spirit, because I found not Titus my brother: but taking my leave of them, I went from thence into Macedonia.*

**L. In church discipline, a person can be given to the Devil for the destruction of the flesh so that the spirit might be saved. I Cor. 5:3-5 KJV**

*3For I verily, as absent in body, but present in spirit, have judged already, as though I were present, concerning him that hath so done this deed,*

*5To deliver such an one unto Satan for the destruction of the flesh, that the spirit may be saved in the day of the Lord Jesus.*

## Conclusion

**Philemon 25** *The grace of our Lord Jesus Christ be with your spirit. Amen. KJV*

# KINGDOM OF DARKNESS - ANGELS

## INTRO:

**There are two categories of angels – good or evil angels. This chapter deals with angels of the kingdom of darkness.**

**I. God created both the spirit and earthly creatures in Gen. 2:1 KJV**

*1 Thus the heavens and the earth were finished, and all the host of them.*

a. **Host** SC OT: a mass of persons (or figuratively, things), especially reg. organized for war (an army); by implication, a campaign, literally or figuratively (specifically, hardship, worship)

1. SC OT: a primitive root; to mass (an army or servants)

b. Barnes' Notes - defining host

1. "a host in marching order," a company of persons or things in the order of their nature and the progressive discharge of their functions. Hence, it is applied to;

| | | |
|---|---|---|
| **a.** | The starry host | Deut. 4:19 |
| **b.** | The angelic host | 1 Kings 22:19 |
| **c.** | The host of Israel | Ex. 12:41 |
| **d.** | The ministering Levites | Num. 4:23 |

**A. We do not know the exact day that the angels were created – but Job gives us a thought Job 38:4-7 AMP**

*4 Where were you when I laid the foundation of the earth? Declare to Me, if you have and know understanding.*
*5 Who determined the measures of the earth, if you know? Or who stretched the measuring line upon it?*
*6 Upon what were the foundations of it fastened, or who laid its cornerstone,*
*7 When the morning stars sang together and all the sons of God shouted for joy?*

1. **The morning stars were Lucifer and Jesus Isa. 14:12 KJV**

*12 How art thou fallen from heaven, O Lucifer, son of the morning! how art thou cut down to the ground, which didst weaken the nations!*

a. **Lucifer SC OT:** (in the sense of brightness); the morning-star

**Rev. 22:16** *I Jesus have sent mine angel to testify unto you these things in the churches. I am the root and the offspring of David, and the bright and morning star. KJV*

2. **The sons of God refer to the angels of God since man was not created until the sixth day Gen. 1:26 KJV**

*26 And God said, Let us make man in our image, after our likeness: and let them have dominion over the fish of the sea, and over the fowl of the air, and over the cattle, and over all the earth, and over every creeping thing that creepeth upon the earth.*

**Ps. 148:1-5 KJV**
*1 Praise ye the LORD. Praise ye the LORD from the heavens: praise him in the heights.*
*2 Praise ye him, all his angels: praise ye him, all his hosts.*
*3 Praise ye him, sun and moon: praise him, all ye stars of light.*
*4 Praise him, ye heavens of heavens, and ye waters that be above the heavens.*
*5 Let them praise the name of the LORD: for he commanded, and they were created.*

B. **Jesus created all of the spirit beings for His ultimate purpose. Col. 1:15-17 AMP**

*15[Now] He is the exact likeness of the unseen God [the visible representation of the invisible]; He is the Firstborn of all creation.*
*16 For it was in Him that all things were created, in heaven and on earth, things seen and things unseen, whether thrones, dominions, rulers, or authorities; all things were created and exist through Him [by His service, intervention] and in and for Him.*
*17 And He Himself existed before all things, and in Him all things consist (cohere, are held together). [Pro. 8:22-31.]*

II. **Evil angels did not exist until Lucifer exalted himself, and drew a third of the angels to follow him. Rev. 12:3-9 KJV**

*3 And there appeared another wonder in heaven; and behold a great red dragon, having seven heads and ten horns, and seven crowns upon his heads.*
*4 And his tail drew the third part of the stars of heaven, and did cast them to the earth: and the dragon stood before the woman which was ready to be delivered, for to devour her child as soon as it was born.*
*5 And she brought forth a man child, who was to rule all nations with a rod of iron: and her child was caught up unto God, and to his throne.*
*6 And the woman fled into the wilderness, where she hath a place prepared of God, that they should feed her there a thousand two hundred and threescore days.*

*7 And there was war in heaven: Michael and his angels fought against the dragon; and the dragon fought and his angels,*
*8 And prevailed not; neither was their place found any more in heaven.*
*9 And the great dragon was cast out, that old serpent, called the Devil, and Satan, which deceiveth the whole world: he was cast out into the earth, and his angels were cast out with him.*

## III. Satan, his followers, the evil angels

### A. Satan was originally called Lucifer Ezek. 28:11-19 TLB

*11 Then this further message came to me from the Lord:*
*12 "Son of dust, weep for the king of Tyre. Tell him, 'The Lord God says: You were the perfection of wisdom and beauty.*
*13 You were in Eden, the garden of God; your clothing was bejeweled with every precious stone-ruby, topaz, diamond, chrysolite, onyx, jasper, sapphire, carbuncle, and emerald-all in beautiful settings of finest gold. They were given to you on the day you were created.*
*14 I appointed you to be the anointed Guardian Angel. You had access to the holy mountain of God. You walked among the stones of fire.*
*15 "'You were perfect in all you did from the day you were created until that time when wrong was found in you.*
*16 Your great wealth filled you with internal turmoil, and you sinned. Therefore, I cast you out of the mountain of God like a common sinner. I destroyed you, O Guardian Angel, from the midst of the stones of fire.*
*17 Your heart was filled with pride because of all your beauty; you corrupted your wisdom for the sake of your splendor. Therefore, I have cast you down to the ground and exposed you helpless before the curious gaze of kings.*
*18 You defiled your holiness with lust for gain; therefore, I brought forth fire from your own actions and let it burn you to ashes upon the earth in the sight of all those watching you.*
*19 All who know you are appalled at your fate; you are an example of horror; you are destroyed forever.'"*

### B. Satan became a king over the kingdom of darkness Rev. 9:11 KJV

*11 And they had a king over them, which is the angel of the bottomless pit, whose name in the Hebrew tongue is Abaddon, but in the Greek tongue hath his name Apollyon.*

**Matt. 12:25-26 KJV**
*25 And Jesus knew their thoughts, and said unto them, Every kingdom divided against itself is brought to desolation; and every city or house divided against itself shall not stand:*
*26 And if Satan cast out Satan, he is divided against himself; how shall then his kingdom stand?*

**Col. 1:13** *[The Father] has delivered and drawn us to Himself out of the control and the dominion of darkness and has transferred us into the kingdom of the Son of His love, AMP*

### C. Satan also took one-third of the angels of heaven with him Rev. 12:3-4 KJV

*3 And there appeared another wonder in heaven; and behold a great red dragon, having seven heads and ten horns, and seven crowns upon his heads.*

*4 And his tail drew the third part of the stars of heaven, and did cast them to the earth: and the dragon stood before the woman which was ready to be delivered, for to devour her child as soon as it was born.*

1. **Some of the angels are called fallen angels**

   **Jude 6** *And the angels which kept not their first estate, but left their own habitation, he hath reserved in everlasting chains under darkness unto the judgment of the great day. KJV*

   **2 Pet. 2:4** *For if God spared not the angels that sinned, but cast them down to hell, and delivered them into chains of darkness, to be reserved unto judgment; KJV*

2. **Evil spirits Acts 19:12 KJV**

   *12 So that from his body were brought unto the sick handkerchiefs or aprons, and the diseases departed from them, and the evil spirits went out of them.*

3. **Some are called devils Matt. 4:24 KJV**

   *24 And his fame went throughout all Syria: and they brought unto him all sick people that were taken with divers diseases and torments, and those which were possessed with devils, and those which were lunatick, and those that had the palsy; and he healed them.*

   a. **Devils** SC NT: to be exercised by a daemon:

      1. *SC NT: 1142 (to distribute fortunes); a daemon or supernatural spirit (of a bad nature)*

**D. The Bible gives many descriptions of the demons of Satan's kingdom**

1. **Evil Spirits Acts 19:13 KJV**

   *13 Then certain of the vagabond Jews, exorcists, took upon them to call over them which had evil spirits the name of the Lord Jesus, saying, We adjure you by Jesus whom Paul preacheth.*

2. **Seducing Spirits I Tim. 4:1 KJV**

   *1 Now the Spirit speaketh expressly, that in the latter times some shall depart from the faith, giving heed to seducing spirits, and doctrines of devils;*

3. **Lying Spirit 1 Kings 22:21-23 KJV**

   *21 And there came forth a spirit, and stood before the LORD, and said, I will persuade him.*
   *22 And the LORD said unto him, Wherewith? And he said, I will go forth, and I will be a lying spirit in the mouth of all his prophets. And he said, Thou shalt persuade him, and prevail also: go forth, and do so.*

*23 Now therefore, behold, the LORD hath put a lying spirit in the mouth of all these thy prophets, and the LORD hath spoken evil concerning thee.*

4. **Unclean Spirit Matt. 12:43 KJV**

*43 When the unclean spirit is gone out of a man, he walketh through dry places, seeking rest, and findeth none.*

5. **Foul – Deaf and Dumb Spirit Mark 9:25 KJV**

*25 When Jesus saw that the people came running together, he rebuked the foul spirit, saying unto him, Thou dumb and deaf spirit, I charge thee, come out of him, and enter no more into him.*

6. **Spirit of Infirmity Luke 13:10-11 KJV**

*10 And he was teaching in one of the synagogues on the sabbath.*
*11 And, behold, there was a woman which had a spirit of infirmity eighteen years, and was bowed together, and could in no wise lift up herself.*

7. **Spirit of Divination Acts 16:16 KJV**

*16 And it came to pass, as we went to prayer, a certain damsel possessed with a spirit of divination met us, which brought her masters much gain by soothsaying:*

8. **Familiar Spirit Isa. 29:4 KJV**

*4 And thou shalt be brought down, and shalt speak out of the ground, and thy speech shall be low out of the dust, and thy voice shall be, as of one that hath a familiar spirit, out of the ground, and thy speech shall whisper out of the dust.*

## IV. The good angels

### A. After creation the first mention of an angel involves delivering a message to Hagar Gen. 16:6-11 KJV

*6 But Abram said unto Sarai, Behold, thy maid is in thy hand; do to her as it pleaseth thee. And when Sarai dealt hardly with her, she fled from her face.*
*7 And the angel of the LORD found her by a fountain of water in the wilderness, by the fountain in the way to Shur.*
*8 And he said, Hagar, Sarai's maid, whence camest thou? and whither wilt thou go? And she said, I flee from the face of my mistress Sarai.*
*9 And the angel of the LORD said unto her, Return to thy mistress, and submit thyself under her hands.*
*10 And the angel of the LORD said unto her, I will multiply thy seed exceedingly, that it shall not be numbered for multitude.*
*11 And the angel of the LORD said unto her, Behold, thou art with child, and shalt bear a son, and shalt call his name Ishmael; because the LORD hath heard thy affliction.*

**Gen. 21:17** *And God heard the voice of the lad; and the angel of God called Hagar out of heaven, and said unto her, What aileth thee, Hagar? fear not; for God hath heard the voice of the lad where he is. KJV*

1. **Angel** SC OT: to despatch as a deputy; a messenger; specifically, of God, i.e. an angel (also a prophet, priest or teacher)

**Heb. 1:13-14 KJV**
*13 But to which of the angels said he at any time, Sit on my right hand, until I make thine enemies thy footstool?*
*14 Are they not all ministering spirits, sent forth to minister for them who shall be heirs of salvation?*

**Ps. 103:20** *Bless the LORD, ye his angels, that excel in strength, that do his commandments, hearkening unto the voice of his word. KJV*

**B. The second ministry of the good angels is to worship God. Rev. 5:11-14 KJV**

*11 And I beheld, and I heard the voice of many angels round about the throne and the beasts and the elders: and the number of them was ten thousand times ten thousand, and thousands of thousands;*
*12 Saying with a loud voice, Worthy is the Lamb that was slain to receive power, and riches, and wisdom, and strength, and honour, and glory, and blessing.*
*13 And every creature which is in heaven, and on the earth, and under the earth, and such as are in the sea, and all that are in them, heard I saying, Blessing, and honour, and glory, and power, be unto Him that sitteth upon the throne, and unto the Lamb forever and ever.*
*14 And the four beasts said, Amen. And the four and twenty elders fell down and worshipped him that liveth forever and ever.*

**C. Read the book of Revelation and you will see the ministry of angels fulfilling God's purpose for humanity and end times**

# THE PERSON

## INTRO:

**The Holy Spirit is the third person in the Godhead. The scriptures reveal the person, work, and ministry of the Holy Spirit. All books of the New Testament except II & III John make reference to the Holy Spirit.**

**I. The Word of God reveals to us the Holy Spirit as a separate expression of the person of God. There are many scriptures that reveal the Father, Son, and Holy Spirit as individuals Matt. 3:16-17 KJV**

*16 And Jesus, when he was baptized, went up straightway out of the water: and, lo, the heavens were opened unto him, and he saw the Spirit of God descending like a dove, and lighting upon him:*
*17 And lo a voice from heaven, saying, This is my beloved Son, in whom I am well pleased.*

**John 14:16** *And I will pray the Father, and he shall give you another Comforter, that he may abide with you forever; KJV*

1. Another Comforter does not mean something different in character, attributes, or adding to who Jesus was – rather the Comforter is to be exactly like Jesus

**John 14:26** *But the Comforter, which is the Holy Ghost, whom the Father will send in my name, he shall teach you all things, and bring all things to your remembrance, whatsoever I have said unto you. KJV*

**II. The Holy Spirit demonstrates 9 personal characteristics that reveal his personhood.**

**A. The Holy Spirit has a mind Rom. 8:27 KJV**

*27 And he that searcheth the hearts knoweth what is the mind of the Spirit, because he maketh intercession for the saints according to the will of God.*

1. **Mind** SC NT: (mental) inclination or purpose

   a. SC NT: to exercise the mind, i.e. entertain or have a sentiment or opinion; by implication, to be (mentally) disposed (more or less earnestly in a certain direction); intensively, to interest oneself in (with concern or obedience)

**B. The Holy Spirit has a will 1 Cor. 12:11 KJV**

*11 But all these worketh that one and the selfsame Spirit, dividing to every man severally as he will.*

**Acts 16:6** *Now when they had gone throughout Phrygia and the region of Galatia, and were forbidden of the Holy Ghost to preach the word in Asia, KJV*

1. **Will** SC NT: verb to "will," i.e. (reflexively) be willing

**C. The Holy Spirit has knowledge 1 Cor. 2:10-11 KJV**

*10 But God hath revealed them unto us by his Spirit: for the Spirit searcheth all things, yea, the deep things of God.*
*11 For what man knoweth the things of a man, save the spirit of man which is in him? even so the things of God knoweth no man, but the Spirit of God.*

**1 Cor. 12:8** *For to one is given by the Spirit the word of wisdom; to another the word of knowledge by the same Spirit; KJV*

**Eph. 1:17** *That the God of our Lord Jesus Christ, the Father of glory, may give unto you the spirit of wisdom and revelation in the knowledge of him: KJV*

**Col. 2:2-3 KJV**
*2 That their hearts might be comforted, being knit together in love, and unto all riches of the full assurance of understanding, to the acknowledgment of the mystery of God, and of the Father, and of Christ;*
*3 In whom are hid all the treasures of wisdom and knowledge.*

**2 Peter 3:18** *But grow in grace, and in the knowledge of our Lord and Saviour Jesus Christ. To him be glory both now and forever. Amen. KJV*

**D. The Holy Spirit has love (Emotions) Rom. 15:30 KJV**

*30 Now I beseech you, brethren, for the Lord Jesus Christ's sake, and for the love of the Spirit, that ye strive together with me in your prayers to God for me;*

**Rom. 5:5** *And hope maketh not ashamed; because the love of God is shed abroad in our hearts by the Holy Ghost_which is given unto us. KJV*

1. **Love** SC NT: love, i.e. affection or benevolence; especially (plural) a love-feast:

**Gal. 5:22-23 KJV**
*22 But the fruit of the Spirit is love, joy, peace, longsuffering, gentleness, goodness, faith,*
*23 Meekness, temperance: against such there is no law.*

1. The Holy Spirit can be grieved or saddened Eph. 4:29-30 KJV

   *29 Let no corrupt communication proceed out of your mouth, but that which is good to the use of edifying, that it may minister grace unto the hearers.*
   *30 And grieve not the Holy Spirit of God, whereby ye are sealed unto the day of redemption.*

   a. **Grieve** SC NT: to distress; reflexively or passively, to be sad

2. Compassion was constantly flowing through Christ as He ministered with the anointing of the Holy Spirit. The word compassion is defined as follows:

   a. **Compassion** SC NT: to have the bowels yearn, i.e. (figuratively) feel sympathy, to pity

      1. SC NT: (the "spleen"); an intestine (plural); figuratively, pity or sympathy

3. Compassion can be a driving emotion that motivates one to action

   a. Jesus and the multitudes Matt. 9:36 KJV

      *36 But when he saw the multitudes, he was moved with compassion on them, because they fainted, and were scattered abroad, as sheep having no shepherd.*

   b. Multitudes – healing their sick Matt. 14:14 KJV

      *14 And Jesus went forth, and saw a great multitude, and was moved with compassion toward them, and he healed their sick.*

   c. Multitudes followed him – there desire over-rode their hunger Matt. 15:32 KJV

      *32 Then Jesus called his disciples unto him, and said, I have compassion on the multitude, because they continue with me now three days, and have nothing to eat: and I will not send them away fasting, lest they faint in the way.*

   d. Jesus heals the blind – they receive their sight Matt. 20:34 KJV

      *34 So Jesus had compassion on them, and touched their eyes: and immediately their eyes received sight, and they followed him.*

   e. Jesus cleanses the leper Mark 1:41 KJV

      *41 And Jesus, moved with compassion, put forth his hand, and touched him, and saith unto him, I will; be thou clean.*

4. The believers are to demonstrate compassion one to another 1 Peter 3:8 KJV

*8 Finally, be ye all of one mind, having compassion one of another, love as brethren, be pitiful, be courteous:*

   a. **Compassion** SC NT: having a fellow-feeling ("sympathetic"), i.e. (by implication) mutually commiserative

      1. SC NT: to experience pain jointly or of the same kind (specifically, persecution; to "sympathize")

      2. SC NT: a primary verb; to experience a sensation or impression (usually painful)

**E. The Holy Spirit intercedes - prays for the saints Rom. 8:26-27 KJV**

*26 Likewise the Spirit also helpeth our infirmities: for we know not what we should pray for as we ought: but the Spirit itself maketh intercession for us with groaning which cannot be uttered.*
*27 And he that searcheth the hearts knoweth what is the mind of the Spirit, because he maketh intercession for the saints according to the will of God.*

1. **Intercede** SC NT: to intercede in behalf of

   a. SC NT: to chance upon, i.e. (by implication) confer with; by extension to entreat (in favor or against):

   b. SC NT: to make ready or bring to pass is used in certain tenses;

      1. The idea of effecting; properly, to affect

      2. Or (specifically) to hit or light upon (as a mark to be reached)

      3. To attain or secure an object or end

      4. To happen (as if meeting with)

**F. The Holy Spirit has intelligence and goodness Neh. 9:20 KJV**

*20 Thou gavest also thy good spirit to instruct them, and withheldest not thy manna from their mouth, and gavest them water for their thirst.*

1. **Good** SC OT: good (as an adjective) in the widest sense; used likewise as a noun, (good, a good or good thing, a good man or woman; the good, goods or good things, good men or women), also as an adverb (well)

2. **Instruct** SC OT: to be (causatively, make or act) circumspect and hence, intelligent

## G. The Holy Spirit has no vocal cords, tongue, or lips yet he speaks

**Matt. 10:20** *For it is not ye that speak, but the Spirit of your Father which speaketh in you. KJV*

**Ezek. 11:5** *And the Spirit of the LORD fell upon me, and said unto me, Speak; Thus saith the LORD; Thus have ye said, O house of Israel: for I know the things that come into your mind, every one of them. KJV*

**Rev. 2:7-11-29; 3:6-13-22 KJV**

**Rev. 2:7** *He that hath an ear, let him hear what the Spirit saith unto the churches; To him that overcometh will I give to eat of the tree of life, which is in the midst of the paradise of God.*

**Acts 20:22-23 AMP**

*22 And now, you see, I am going to Jerusalem, bound by the [Holy] Spirit and obligated and compelled by the [convictions of my own] spirit, not knowing what will befall me there—*

*23 Except that the Holy Spirit clearly and emphatically affirms to me in city after city that imprisonment and suffering await me.*

**I Tim. 4:1** *Now the Spirit speaketh expressly, that in the latter times some shall depart from the faith, giving heed to seducing spirits, and doctrines of devils; KJV*

1. **Speaketh** SC NT properly, to "lay" forth, i.e. (figuratively)_relate (in words [usually of systematic or set discourse

   **Jn. 16:13** *Howbeit when he, the Spirit of truth, is come, he will guide you into all truth: for he shall not speak of himself; but whatsoever he shall hear, that shall he speak: and he will shew you things to come. (KJV)*

## H. The Holy Spirit has no physical ears yet he can hear John 16:13 KJV

*13 Howbeit when he, the Spirit of truth, is come, he will guide you into all truth: for he shall not speak of himself; but whatsoever he shall hear, that shall he speak: and he will shew you things to come.*

1. The Holy Spirit lives within the believer. Because He lives within the same body as ourselves He has access to our minds and thought life. He knows all of our thoughts.

## I. The Holy Spirit can be fellowshipped with Phil. 2:1 KJV

*1 If there be therefore any consolation in Christ, if any comfort of love, if any fellowship of the Spirit, if any bowels and mercies,*

1. **Fellowship** SC NT: partnership, i.e. (literally) participation, or (social) intercourse, or (pecuniary) benefaction:

**a.** SC NT: a sharer i.e. associate

**b.** SC NT: common, i.e. (literally) shared by all or several, or (cer.) profane

**c.** SC NT: a primary preposition denoting union; with or together by association, companionship, process, resemblance, possession, instrumentality, addition

**2 Cor. 13:14** *The grace of the Lord Jesus Christ, and the love of God, and the communion of the Holy Ghost, be with you all. Amen. KJV*

# ACTIONS (1-26)

## INTRO:

**The actions of the Holy Spirit are activities that work as benefits to the believer. These individual experiences propel the believer in his or her walk with God. The actions of the Holy Spirit are as follows:**

1. **The Spirit will lead you into the purposes of God for your life**

   a. Jesus was led by the Spirit into the wilderness to be tempted of the Devil Matt. 4:1 KJV

      *1 Then was Jesus led up of the Spirit into the wilderness to be tempted of the devil.*

      1. **Led** SC NT: to lead up; by extension to bring out; specially, to sail away

   b. Jesus was led into the council of the elders, scribes, and chief priests Luke 22:66 KJV

      *66 And as soon as it was day, the elders of the people and the chief priests and the scribes came together, and led him into their council, saying,*

   c. When we are led by the Spirit it speaks to us of being in relationship as a son of God Rom. 8:14 KJV

      *14 For as many as are led by the Spirit of God, they are the sons of God.*

      1. **Led** SC NT: a primary verb; properly, to lead; by implication, to bring, drive(reflexively) go, (specially) pass (time), or (figuratively) induce

2. **The Spirit can drive or expel you into the purpose of God Mark 1:12 KJV**

   *12 And immediately the Spirit driveth him into the wilderness.*

   a. **Drive** SC NT: to eject (literally or figuratively)

3. **The Spirit sends individuals to fulfill a mission Isa. 48:16 KJV**

*16 Come ye near unto me, hear ye this; I have not spoken in secret from the beginning; from the time that it was, there am I: and now the Lord GOD, and his Spirit, hath sent me.*

**Acts 13:2-4 KJV**

*2 As they ministered to the Lord, and fasted, the Holy Ghost said, Separate me Barnabas and Saul for the work where unto I have called them.*

*3 And when they had fasted and prayed, and laid their hands on them, they sent them away.*

*4 So they, being sent forth by the Holy Ghost, departed unto Seleucia; and from thence they sailed to Cyprus.*

**a. Sent** SC NT: to despatch

**4. The Spirit directs our lives in specific ways to accomplish His will**

**a.** Philip and the Ethiopian eunuch Acts 8:26-30 KJV

*26 And the angel of the Lord spake unto Philip, saying, Arise, and go toward the south unto the way that goeth down from Jerusalem unto Gaza, which is desert.*

*27 And he arose and went: and, behold, a man of Ethiopia, an eunuch of great authority under Candace queen of the Ethiopians, who had the charge of all her treasure, and had come to Jerusalem for to worship,*

*28 Was returning, and sitting in his chariot read Esaias the prophet.*

*29 Then the Spirit said unto Philip, Go near, and join thyself to this chariot.*

*30 And Philip ran thither to him, and heard him read the prophet Esaias, and said, Understandest thou what thou readest?*

**b.** Peter is directed to go to Caesarea unto a man called Cornelius – Read the whole account in Acts 10:1-49 – As you read the account take note of the specific instructions which were given to both Peter and Cornelius

*1 There was a certain man in Caesarea called Cornelius, a centurion of the band called the Italian band, KJV*

**Acts 10:19** *While Peter thought on the vision, the Spirit said unto him, Behold, three men seek thee. KJV*

**c.** Paul and Silas had to make adjustments in the places of ministry

**Acts 15:40-41 KJV**

*40 And Paul chose Silas, and departed, being recommended by the brethren unto the grace of God.*

*41 And he went through Syria and Cilicia, confirming the churches.*

**Acts 16:6-8 KJV**

*6 Now when they had gone throughout Phrygia and the region of Galatia, and were forbidden of the Holy Ghost to preach the word in Asia,*

*7 After they were come to Mysia, they assayed to go into Bithynia: but the Spirit suffered them not.*

*8 And they passing by Mysia came down to Troas.*

5. **The Spirit calls into service – setting limits and boundaries of the ministry Acts 13:1-2 KJV**

*1 Now there were in the church that was at Antioch certain prophets and teachers; as Barnabas, and Simeon that was called Niger, and Lucius of Cyrene, and Manaen, which had been brought up with Herod the tetrarch, and Saul.*
*2 As they ministered to the Lord, and fasted, the Holy Ghost said, Separate me Barnabas and Saul for the work where unto I have called them.*

a. **Separate** SC NT: to set off by boundary, i.e. (figuratively) limit, exclude, appoint

b. **Paul** **2 Tim. 1:11** *Whereunto I am appointed a preacher, and an apostle, and a teacher of the Gentiles. KJV*

**Eph. 3:8** *Unto me, who am less than the least of all saints, is this grace given, that I should preach among the Gentiles the unsearchable riches of Christ; KJV*

c. **Peter** **Gal. 2:7-8 KJV**
*7 But contrariwise, when they saw that the gospel of the uncircumcision was committed unto me, as the gospel of the circumcision was unto Peter;*
*8(For he that wrought effectually in Peter to the apostleship of the circumcision, the same was mighty in me toward the Gentiles:*

6. **The Spirit gives rest or settling down Isa. 63:14 KJV**

*14 As a beast goeth down into the valley, the Spirit of the LORD caused him to rest: so didst thou lead thy people, to make thyself a glorious name.*

a. **Rest** SC OT: to rest, i.e. settle down; used in a great variety of applications, (to dwell, stay, let fall, place, let alone, withdraw, give comfort, etc.)

7. **The Spirit can transport you into spiritual experiences Ezek. 11:24 KJV**

*24 Afterwards the spirit took me up, and brought me in a vision by the Spirit of God into Chaldea, to them of the captivity. So the vision that I had seen went up from me.*

**Ezek. 37:1** *The hand of the LORD was upon me, and carried me out in the spirit of the LORD, and set me down in the midst of the valley which was full of bones, KJV*

**Ezek. 43:4-6 KJV**
*4 And the glory of the LORD came into the house by the way of the gate whose prospect is toward the east.*
*5 So the spirit took me up, and brought me into the inner court; and, behold, the glory of the LORD filled the house.*
*6 And I heard him speaking unto me out of the house; and the man stood by me.*

**Acts 8:39-40 KJV**

*39 And when they were come up out of the water, the Spirit of the Lord caught away Philip, that the eunuch saw him no more: and he went on his way rejoicing.*
*40 But Philip was found at Azotus: and passing through he preached in all the cities, till he came to Caesarea.*

8. **The Spirit gives power which is a force to complete a task Mic. 3:8 KJV**

*8 But truly I am full of power by the spirit of the LORD, and of judgment, and of might, to declare unto Jacob his transgression, and to Israel his sin.*

   a. **Power** SC OT: to be firm; vigor, literally (force) or figuratively (capacity, means, produce); also (from its hardiness) a large lizard

9. **The Spirit also gives miraculous power to make possible miraculous happenings Acts 1:8 KJV**

*8 But ye shall receive power, after that the Holy Ghost is come upon you: and ye shall be witnesses unto me both in Jerusalem, and in all Judaea, and in Samaria, and unto the uttermost part of the earth.*

   a. **Power** SC NT: force (literally or figuratively); specially, miraculous power (usually by implication, a miracle itself)

      1. **Power** SC NT: to be able or possible

10. **The Spirit empowers for the removal of evil spirits Matt. 12:28 KJV**

*28 But if I cast out devils by the Spirit of God, then the kingdom of God is come unto you.*

11. **The Spirit testifies of Jesus John 15:26 KJV**

*26 But when the Comforter is come, whom I will send unto you from the Father, even the Spirit of truth, which proceedeth from the Father, he shall testify of me:*

   a. **Testify** SC NT: to be witness, i.e. testify (literally or figuratively)

12. **The Spirit will teach all things concerning the Word of God. He will remind you by bringing the Word to your memory John 14:26 KJV**

*26 But the Comforter, which is the Holy Ghost, whom the Father will send in my name, he shall teach you all things, and bring all things to your remembrance, whatsoever I have said unto you.*

   a. **Teaches** SC NT: (to learn); to teach (in the same broad application)

   b. **Bring/Remembrance** SC NT: to remind quietly, i.e. suggest to the (middle voice one's own) memory

**1 Cor. 2:13** *Which things also we speak, not in the words which man's wisdom teacheth, but which the Holy Ghost teacheth; comparing spiritual things with spiritual. KJV*

**13. The Spirit reproves the world of sin, righteousness, and judgment John 16:7-11 KJV**

*7 Nevertheless I tell you the truth; It is expedient for you that I go away: for if I go not away, the Comforter will not come unto you; but if I depart, I will send him unto you.*
*8 And when he is come, he will reprove the world of sin, and of righteousness, and of judgment:*
*9 Of sin, because they believe not on me;*
*10 Of righteousness, because I go to my Father, and ye see me no more;*
*11 Of judgment, because the prince of this world is judged.*

a. **Reprove** SC NT: to confute, admonish

**14. The Spirit guides you into all truth John 16:13 KJV**

*13 Howbeit when he, the Spirit of truth, is come, he will guide you into all truth: for he shall not speak of himself; but whatsoever he shall hear, that shall he speak: and he will shew you things to come.*

a. **Guide** SC NT: to show the way (literally or figuratively [teach])

   1. SC NT: a conductor (literally or figuratively [teacher])

   2. SC NT: to lead, i.e. command (with official authority)

**15. The Spirit will shew you things to come John 16:13 KJV**

a. **Shows** SC NT: to announce (in detail)

**16. The Spirit glorifies Jesus by receiving from him and showing it to you John 16:14 KJV**

*14 He shall glorify me: for he shall receive of mine, and shall shew it unto you.*

a. **Glorify** SC NT: to render (or esteem) glorious (in a wide application)

   1. SC NT: glory as very apparent

**17. The Spirit searches all things I Cor. 2:10 KJV**

*10 But God hath revealed them unto us by his Spirit: for the Spirit searcheth all things, yea, the deepthings of God.*

a. **Searcheth** SC NT: (through the idea of inquiry); to seek, i.e. (figuratively) to investigate

b. **Deep** SC NT: profundity, i.e. (by implication) extent; (figuratively) mystery

c. **Profundity** - Great depth, Depth of intellect, feeling, or meaning; something profound or abstruse

d. **Vines SEARCH**

1. "To search, examine," is used

2. Of God, as "searching" the heart, **Rom. 8:27 KJV**

*27 And he that searcheth the hearts knoweth what is the mind of the Spirit, because he maketh intercession for the saints according to the will of God.*

3. Of Christ, **Rev. 2:23 KJV**

*23 And I will kill her children with death; and all the churches shall know that I am he which searcheth the reins and hearts: and I will give unto every one of you according to your works.*

4. Of the Holy Spirit, as "searching" all things, **I Cor. 2:10 KJV**

*10 But God hath revealed them unto us by his Spirit: for the Spirit searcheth all things, yea, the deep things of God.*

5. Acting in the spirit of the believer. **I Pet. 1:11 KJV**

*11 Searching what, or what manner of time the Spirit of Christ which was in them did signify, when it testified beforehand the sufferings of Christ, and the glory that should follow.*

**18. The Spirit will quicken or revitalize our mortal bodies Rom. 8:11 KJV**

*11 But if the Spirit of him that raised up Jesus from the dead dwell in you, he that raised up Christ from the dead shall also quicken your mortal bodies by his Spirit that dwelleth in you.*

a. **Quicken** SC NT; (re-) vitalize (literally or figuratively)

**19. The Spirit will aid you in killing the deeds of the old life Rom. 8:13 KJV**

*13 For if ye live after the flesh, ye shall die: but if ye through the Spirit do mortify the deeds of the body, ye shall live.*

a. **Mortify** SC NT: to kill (literally or figuratively)

**Col. 3:5** *Mortify therefore your members which are upon the earth; fornication, uncleanness, inordinate affection, evil concupiscence, and covetousness, which is idolatry: KJV*

1. **Mortify** SC NT: to deaden, i.e. (figuratively) to subdue

    a. SC NT: (a corpse); dead (literally or figuratively; also as a noun)

**20. The Spirit will bear witness with our spirit that we are the children of God Rom. 8:15-16 KJV**

*15 For ye have not received the spirit of bondage again to fear; but ye have received the Spirit of adoption, whereby we cry, Abba, Father.*
*16 The Spirit itself beareth witness with our spirit, that we are the children of God:*

**21. The Spirit helps our infirmities or weakness through interceding for us Rom. 8:26-27 KJV**

*26 Likewise the Spirit also helpeth our infirmities: for we know not what we should pray for as we ought: but the Spirit itself maketh intercession for us with groanings which cannot be uttered.*
*27 And he that searcheth the hearts knoweth what is the mind of the Spirit, because he maketh intercession for the saints according to the will of God.*

a. **Infirmities** SC NT: feebleness (of mind or body); by implication, malady; morally, frailty

    1. SC NT: strength less (in various applications, literal, figurative, and moral)

**22. The Spirit will demonstrate the wonderworking of God 1 Cor. 2:4 KJV**

*4 And my speech and my preaching was not with enticing words of man's wisdom, but in demonstration of the Spirit and of power:*

a. **Demonstration** SC NT: manifestation

    1. SC NT: to show off, i.e. exhibit; figuratively, to demonstrate, i.e. accredit

**23. The Spirit will manifest through the following ways 1 Cor. 12:4-11 KJV**

*4 Now there are diversities of gifts, but the same Spirit.*
*5 And there are differences of administrations, but the same Lord.*
*6 And there are diversities of operations, but it is the same God which worketh all in all.*
*7 But the manifestation of the Spirit is given to every man to profit withal.*

a. **Manifestation** SC NT: 5321 exhibition, i.e. (figuratively) expression, (by extension) a bestowment

    1. SC NT: to render apparent (literally or figuratively)

    2. SC NT: shining, i.e. apparent (literally or figuratively); neuter (as adverb) publicly, externally

*8 For to one is given by the Spirit the word of wisdom; to another the word of knowledge by the same Spirit;*
*9 To another faith by the same Spirit; to another the gifts of healing by the same Spirit;*
*10 To another the working of miracles; to another prophecy; to another discerning of spirits; to another divers kinds of tongues; to another the interpretation of tongues:*
*11 But all these worketh that one and the selfsame Spirit, dividing to every man severally as he will.*

**24. The Spirit writes upon the tables of our heart 2 Cor. 3:3 KJV**

*3 Forasmuch as ye are manifestly declared to be the epistle of Christ ministered by us, written not with ink, but with the Spirit of the living God; not in tables of stone, but in fleshy tables of the heart.*

a. **Written** SC NT: to "engrave", i.e. inscribe

**25. The Spirit gives life 2 Cor. 3:6 KJV**

*6 Who also hath made us able ministers of the New Testament; not of the letter, but of the spirit: for the letter killeth, but the spirit giveth life.*

**John 6:63** *It is the spirit that quickeneth; the flesh profiteth nothing: the words that I speak unto you, they are spirit, and they are life. KJV*

**26. The Spirit gives liberty. 2 Cor. 3:17 KJV**

*17 Now the Lord is that Spirit: and where the Spirit of the Lord is, there is liberty.*

a. **Liberty** SC NT: freedom (legitimate or licentious, chiefly moral or ceremonial)

   1. SC NT: unrestrained (to go at pleasure), i.e. (as a citizen) not a slave (whether freeborn or manumitted), or (genitive case) exempt (from obligation or liability):

# ACTIONS (27-52)

## INTRO:

**The actions of the Holy Spirit are activities that work as benefits to the believer. These individual experiences propel the believer in his or her walk with God. The actions of the Holy Spirit are as follows:**

**27. The Spirit is building us together for a permanent dwelling place of God Eph. 2:20-22 KJV**

*20 And are built upon the foundation of the apostles and prophets, Jesus Christ himself being the chief cornerstone;*
*21 In whom all the building fitly framed together groweth unto an holy temple in the Lord:*
*22 In whom ye also are builded together for an habitation of God through the Spirit.*

1. **Are builded together** SC NT: to construct, i.e. (passively) to compose (in company with other Christians, figuratively)

    a. SC NT: 4862 sun (soon); a primary preposition denoting union; with or together

    b. SC NT: to be a house-builder, i.e. construct or (figuratively) confirm

2. **Habitation** SC NT: a dwelling-place

    a. SC NT: to house permanently, i.e. reside (literally or figuratively)

**28. The Spirit reveals the secrets of God Eph. 3:4-6 KJV**

*4 Whereby, when ye read, ye may understand my knowledge in the mystery of Christ)*
*5 Which in other ages was not made known unto the sons of men, as it is now revealed unto his holy apostles and prophets by the Spirit;*
*6 That the Gentiles should be fellow heirs, and of the same body, and partakers of his promise in Christ by the gospel:*

**29. The Spirit strengthens the inner man Eph. 3:16 KJV**

*16 That he would grant you, according to the riches of his glory, to be strengthened with might by his Spirit in the inner man;*

1. **Strengthened** SC NT: to empower, i.e. (passively) increase in vigor

   a. SC NT: powerful

   b. SC NT: vigor ["great"] (literally or figuratively)

**30. The Spirit sanctifies or makes one pure 2 Thess. 2:13 KJV**

*13 But we are bound to give thanks alway to God for you, brethren beloved of the Lord, because God hath from the beginning chosen you to salvation through sanctification of the Spirit and belief of the truth:*

**1 Pet. 1:2** *Elect according to the foreknowledge of God the Father, through sanctification of the Spirit, unto obedience and sprinkling of the blood of Jesus Christ: Grace unto you, and peace, be multiplied. KJV*

a. **Sanctification** SC NT: properly, purification, i.e. (the state) purity; concretely (by Hebraism) a purifier

   1. SC NT: to make holy, i.e. (ceremonially) purify or consecrate; (mentally) to venerate

   2. SC NT: sacred (physically, pure, morally blameless or religious, ceremonially, consecrated)

**31. The Spirit gives self-control 2 Tim. 1:7 KJV**

*7 For God hath not given us the spirit of fear; but of power, and of love, and of a sound mind.*

**32. The Spirit helps us to obey the truth I Pet. 1:22 KJV**

*22 Seeing ye have purified your souls in obeying the truth through the Spirit unto unfeigned love of the brethren, see that ye love one another with a pure heart fervently:*

**33. The Spirit brings about regeneration John 3:5-6 KJV**

*5 Jesus answered, Verily, verily, I say unto thee, Except a man be born of water and of the Spirit, he cannot enter into the kingdom of God.*
*6 That which is born of the flesh is flesh; and that which is born of the Spirit is spirit.*

**Titus 3:5** *Not by works of righteousness which we have done, but according to his mercy he saved us, by the washing of regeneration, and renewing of the Holy Ghost; KJV*

a. **Regeneration** SC NT: (spiritual) rebirth (the state or the act), i.e. (figuratively) spiritual renovation; specifically, Messianic restoration

b. **Renewing** SC NT: renovation

**c.** A man must be born of water and of the spirit. John 3:3-5 KJV

**d.** For by one Spirit are we all baptized into one body I Cor. 12:13 KJV

**34. The Spirit strives with men Gen. 6:3 KJV**

*3 And the LORD said, My spirit shall not always strive with man, for that he also is flesh: yet his days shall be an hundred and twenty years.*

**a.** Strive SC OT: to rule; by implication to judge (as umpire); also to strive (as at law)

**35. The Spirit gives the assurance of salvation Rom. 8:15-17 KJV**

*15 For ye have not received the spirit of bondage again to fear; but ye have received the Spirit of adoption, whereby we cry, Abba, Father.*
*16 The Spirit itself beareth witness with our spirit, that we are the children of God:*
*17 And if children, then heirs; heirs of God, and joint-heirs with Christ; if so be that we suffer with him, that we may be also glorified together.*

**a.** **Bears Witness** SC NT: to testify jointly, i.e. corroborate by (concurrent) evidence

**36. The Spirit imparts spiritual gifts 1 Cor. 12:4-7 KJV**

*4 Now there are diversities of gifts, but the same Spirit.*
*5 And there are differences of administrations, but the same Lord.*
*6 And there are diversities of operations, but it is the same God which worketh all in all.*
*7 But the manifestation of the Spirit is given to every man to profit withal.*

**1 Tim. 4:14** *Neglect not the gift that is in thee, which was given thee by prophecy, with the laying on of the hands of the presbytery. KJV*

**Rom. 1:11** *For I long to see you, that I may impart unto you some spiritual gift, to the end ye may be established; KJV*

**37. The Spirit enables you to worship in spirit and truth John 4:23-24 KJV**

*23 But the hour cometh, and now is, when the true worshippers shall worship the Father in spirit and in truth: for the Father seeketh such to worship him.*
*24 God is a Spirit: and they that worship him must worship him in spirit and in truth.*

**Phil. 3:3** *For we are the circumcision, which worship God in the spirit, and rejoice in Christ Jesus, and have no confidence in the flesh. KJV*

**1 Cor. 14:15** *What is it then? I will pray with the spirit, and I will pray with the understanding also: I will sing with the spirit, and I will sing with the understanding also. KJV*

**a. Spiritual Singing Eph. 5:18-20 KJV**

*18 And be not drunk with wine, wherein is excess; but be filled with the Spirit;*
*19 Speaking to yourselves in psalms and hymns and spiritual songs, singing and making melody in your heart to the Lord;*
*20 Giving thanks always for all things unto God and the Father in the name of our Lord Jesus Christ;*

**Col. 3:16** *Let the word of Christ dwell in you richly in all wisdom; teaching and admonishing one another in psalms and hymns and spiritual songs, singing with grace in your hearts to the Lord. KJV*

**I Cor. 14:15** *What is it then? I will pray with the spirit, and I will pray with the understanding also: I will sing with the spirit, and I will sing with the understanding also. KJV*

**38. The Spirit enables us to speak in unknown tongues Acts 2:4 KJV**

*4 And they were all filled with the Holy Ghost, and began to speak with other tongues, as the Spirit gave them utterance.*

**Acts 10:44-46 KJV**
*44 While Peter yet spake these words, the Holy Ghost fell on all them which heard the word.*
*45 And they of the circumcision which believed were astonished, as many as came with Peter, because that on the Gentiles also was poured out the gift of the Holy Ghost.*
*46 For they heard them speak with tongues, and magnify God. Then answered Peter,*

**Acts 19:6** *And when Paul had laid his hands upon them, the Holy Ghost came on them; and they spake with tongues, and prophesied. KJV*

**39. The Spirit gives us the mind of Christ I Cor. 2:13-16 KJV**

*13 Which things also we speak, not in the words which man's wisdom teacheth, but which the Holy Ghost teacheth; comparing spiritual things with spiritual.*
*14 But the natural man receiveth not the things of the Spirit of God: for they are foolishness unto him: neither can he know them, because they are spiritually discerned.*
*15 But he that is spiritual judgeth all things, yet he himself is judged of no man.*
*16 For who hath known the mind of the Lord, that he may instruct him? But we have the mind of Christ.*

**40. The Spirit will bring about the resurrection and immortality to the believer's body Rom. 8:11 KJV**

*11 But if the Spirit of him that raised up Jesus from the dead dwell in you, he that raised up Christ from the dead shall also quicken your mortal bodies by his Spirit that dwelleth in you.*

**1 Cor. 15:47-54 KJV**

*47 The first man is of the earth, earthy: the second man is the Lord from heaven.*
*48 As is the earthy, such are they also that are earthy: and as is the heavenly, such are they also that are heavenly.*
*49 And as we have borne the image of the earthy, we shall also bear the image of the heavenly.*
*50 Now this I say, brethren, that flesh and blood cannot inherit the kingdom of God; neither doth corruption inherit incorruption.*
*51 Behold, I shew you a mystery; We shall not all sleep, but we shall all be changed,*
*52 In a moment, in the twinkling of an eye, at the last trump: for the trumpet shall sound, and the dead shall be raised incorruptible, and we shall be changed.*
*53 For this corruptible must put on incorruption, and this mortal must put on immortality.*
*54 So when this corruptible shall have put on incorruption, and this mortal shall have put on immortality, then shall be brought to pass the saying that is written, Death is swallowed up in victory.*

**41. The Spirit dwells in our body, the temple of the Holy Spirit 1 Cor. 3:16-17 KJV**

*16 Know ye not that ye are the temple of God, and that the Spirit of God dwelleth in you?*
*17 If any man defile the temple of God, him shall God destroy; for the temple of God is holy, which temple ye are.*

a. **Temple** SC NT: (to dwell); a fane, shrine, temple

   1. SC NT: a sacred place, i.e. the entire precincts

b. You have two persons living in one body - cohabiting

   1. **Dwell** SC NT: to occupy a house, i.e. reside (figuratively, inhabit, remain, inhere); by implication to cohabit

**1 Cor. 6:19** *What? know ye not that your body is the temple of the Holy Ghost which is in you, which ye have of God, and ye are not your own? KJV*

**Rom. 8:9** *But ye are not in the flesh, but in the Spirit, if so be that the Spirit of God dwell in you. Now if any man have not the Spirit of Christ, he is none of his. KJV*

**1 Cor. 6:17** *But he that is joined unto the Lord is one spirit. KJV*

**1 John 3:24** *And he that keepeth his commandments dwelleth in him, and he in him. And hereby we know that he abideth in us, by the Spirit which he hath given us. KJV*

**John 14:17** *Even the Spirit of truth; whom the world cannot receive, because it seeth him not, neither knoweth him: but ye know him; for he dwelleth with you, and shall be in you. KJV*

a. **Dwelleth** SC NT: a primary verb; to stay (in a given place, state, relation, or expectancy)

**John 14:23** *Jesus answered and said unto him, If a man love me, he will keep my words: and my Father will love him, and we will come unto him, and make our abode with him. KJV*

a. **Abode** SC NT: a staying, i.e. residence (the act or the place)

**42. He prays or intercedes for us Rom. 8:26 KJV**

*26 Likewise the Spirit also helpeth our infirmities: for we know not what we should pray for as we ought: but the Spirit itself maketh intercession for us with groanings which cannot be uttered.*

a. **Intercession** SC NT: to intercede in behalf of

**43. The Holy Spirit puts his mark upon us. It is for preservation and security Eph. 1:13-14 KJV**

*13 In whom ye also trusted, after that ye heard the word of truth, the gospel of your salvation: in whom also after that ye believed, ye were sealed with that holy Spirit of promise,*
*14 Which is the earnest of our inheritance until the redemption of the purchased possession, unto the praise of his glory.*

a. **Sealed** SC NT: to stamp (with a signet or private mark) for security or preservation (literally or figuratively); by implication, to keep secret, to attest

   1. SC NT: a signet (as fencing in or protecting from misappropriation); by implication, the stamp impressed (as a mark of privacy, or genuineness), literally or figuratively

**44. He is the Comforter that abides forever John 14:16 KJV**

*16 And I will pray the Father, and he shall give you another Comforter, that he may abide with you forever;*

a. **Comforter** SC NT: another of the same kind

b. **Abides** SC NT: a primary verb; to stay (in a given place, state, relation or expectancy)

**1 Cor. 6:19** *What? know ye not that your body is the temple of the Holy Ghost which is in you, which ye have of God, and ye are not your own? KJV*

**1 Cor. 3:16** *Know ye not that ye are the temple of God, and that the Spirit of God dwelleth in you? KJV*

**Rom. 8:9** *But ye are not in the flesh, but in the Spirit, if so be that the Spirit of God dwell in you. Now if any man have not the Spirit of Christ, he is none of his. KJV*

**45. He illuminates our spiritual understanding I Cor. 2:12-14 KJV**

*12 Now we have received, not the spirit of the world, but the spirit which is of God; that we might know the things that are freely given to us of God.*
*13 Which things also we speak, not in the words which man's wisdom teacheth, but which the Holy Ghost teacheth; comparing spiritual things with spiritual.*
*14 But the natural man receiveth not the things of the Spirit of God: for they are foolishness unto him: neither can he know them, because they are spiritually discerned.*

**46. The Spirit liberates from the law of sin and death Rom. 8:2 KJV**

*2 For the law of the Spirit of life in Christ Jesus hath made me free from the law of sin and death.*

a. **Free** SC NT: to liberate, i.e. (figuratively) to exempt (from moral, ceremonial or mortal liability)

   1. SC NT: unrestrained (to go at pleasure), i.e. (as a citizen) not a slave (whether freeborn or manumitted), or (genitive case) exempt (from obligation or liability)

**47. The Spirit bears fruit in the believer's life Gal. 5:22-24 KJV**

*22 But the fruit of the Spirit is love, joy, peace, longsuffering, gentleness, goodness, faith,*
*23 Meekness, temperance: against such there is no law.*
*24 And they that are Christ's have crucified the flesh with the affections and lusts.*

**48. The Spirit gives access to the Father Eph. 2:18 KJV**

*18 For through him we both have access by one Spirit unto the Father.*

a. **Access** SC NT: admission

**49. The Holy Spirit brings a combination of rest, edification, fear, and comfort to our lives Acts 9:31 KJV**

*31 Then had the churches rest throughout all Judaea and Galilee and Samaria, and were edified; and walking in the fear of the Lord, and in the comfort of the Holy Ghost, were multiplied.*

**50. The Holy Spirit imparts the love of God into our life Rom. 5:1-5 KJV**

*1 Therefore being justified by faith, we have peace with God through our Lord Jesus Christ:*
*2 By whom also we have access by faith into this grace wherein we stand, and rejoice in hope of the glory of God.*
*3 And not only so, but we glory in tribulations also: knowing that tribulation worketh patience;*
*4 And patience, experience; and experience, hope:*
*5 And hope maketh not ashamed; because the love of God is shed abroad in our hearts by the Holy Ghost which is given unto us.*

**51. The Holy Spirit will cause you to abound in hope through his power Rom. 15:13 KJV**

*13 Now the God of hope fill you with all joy and peace in believing, that ye may abound in hope, through the power of the Holy Ghost.*

## 52. The world cannot receive the Holy Spirit John 14:17 KJV

*17 Even the Spirit of truth; whom the world cannot receive, because it seeth him not, neither knoweth him: but ye know him; for he dwelleth with you, and shall be in you.*

**John 14:17** *The Spirit of Truth, Whom the world cannot receive (welcome, take to its heart), because it does not see Him or know and recognize Him. But you know and recognize Him, for He lives with you [constantly] and will be in you. AMP*

# ACTIONS (53-76)

## INTRO:

**The actions of the Holy Spirit are activities that work as benefits to the believer. These individual experiences propel the believer in his or her walk with God. The actions of the Holy Spirit are as follows:**

**53. When you are brought before governing leaders for a testimony against them the Holy Spirit will enable you in your ability to speak Matt. 10:18-20 KJV**

*18 And ye shall be brought before governors and kings for my sake, for a testimony against them and the Gentiles.*
*19 But when they deliver you up, take no thought how or what ye shall speak: for it shall be given you in that same hour what ye shall speak.*
*20 For it is not ye that speak, but the Spirit of your Father which speaketh in you.*

**54. When you cast out evil spirits by the Holy Spirit it is a witness that the kingdom of God is come to you Matt. 12:28 KJV**

*28 But if I cast out devils by the Spirit of God, then the kingdom of God is come unto you.*

**55. The Holy Spirit speaks to your future and brings about the fulfillment of your purpose Luke 2:25-28 KJV**

*25 And, behold, there was a man in Jerusalem, whose name was Simeon; and the same man was just and devout, waiting for the consolation of Israel: and the Holy Ghost was upon him.*
*26 And it was revealed unto him by the Holy Ghost, that he should not see death, before he had seen the Lord's Christ.*
*27 And he came by the Spirit into the temple: and when the parents brought in the child Jesus, to do for him after the custom of the law,*
*28 Then took he him up in his arms,*

**56. Jesus was tested by the Devil. The scripture relates that He returned in the power of the Spirit. The Holy Spirit will cause you to have his power after testing – so many times an individual experiences guilt, exhaustion, and an attitude of defeat – note Jesus returned in the power Luke 4:14 KJV**

*14 And Jesus returned in the power of the Spirit into Galilee: and there went out a fame of him through all the region round about.*

**57. The Holy Spirit anoints you for service Luke 4:18-19 KJV**

*18 The Spirit of the Lord is upon me, because he hath anointed me to preach the gospel to the poor; he hath sent me to heal the brokenhearted, to preach deliverance to the captives, and recovering of sight to the blind, to set at liberty them that are bruised,*
*19 To preach the acceptable year of the Lord.*

**58. The Holy Spirit is a gift that is received by a simple asking for him to come to you Luke 11:13 KJV**

*13 If ye then, being evil, know how to give good gifts unto your children: how much more shall your heavenly Father give the Holy Spirit to them that ask him?*

**59. The Holy Spirit is involved in your new birth John 3:5-8 KJV**

*5 Jesus answered, Verily, verily, I say unto thee, Except a man be born of water and of the Spirit, he cannot enter into the kingdom of God.*
*6 That which is born of the flesh is flesh; and that which is born of the Spirit is spirit.*
*7 Marvel not that I said unto thee, Ye must be born again.*
*8 The wind bloweth where it listeth, and thou hearest the sound thereof, but canst not tell whence it cometh, and whither it goeth: so is every one that is born of the Spirit.*

**60. The Holy Spirit and the Word are directly connected John 6:63 KJV**

*63 It is the spirit that quickeneth; the flesh profiteth nothing: the words that I speak unto you, they are spirit, and they are life.*

**Gen. 1:1-5 KJV**
*1 In the beginning God created the heaven and the earth.*
*2 And the earth was without form, and void; and darkness was upon the face of the deep. And the Spirit of God moved upon the face of the waters.*
*3 And God said, Let there be light: and there was light.*
*4 And God saw the light, that it was good: and God divided the light from the darkness.*
*5 And God called the light Day, and the darkness he called Night. And the evening and the morning were the first day.*

**61. The Holy Spirit is like rivers of living water that pour forth from your innermost being John 7:37-39 KJV**

*37 In the last day, that great day of the feast, Jesus stood and cried, saying, If any man thirst, let him come unto me, and drink.*
*38 He that believeth on me, as the scripture hath said, out of his belly shall flow rivers of living water.*
*39(But this spake he of the Spirit, which they that believe on him should receive: for the Holy Ghost was not yet given; because that Jesus was not yet glorified.)*

**62. The Holy Spirit is a promise fulfilled - It began on the day of Pentecost and continues till Jesus comes again Luke 24:49 KJV**

*49 And, behold, I send the promise of my Father upon you: but tarry ye in the city of Jerusalem, until ye be endued with power from on high.*

a. **Promise** SC NT: an announcement (for information, assent, or pledge; especially a divine assurance of good)

   1. SC NT: to announce upon: (by implication) to engage to do something, to assert something respecting oneself

**Acts 2:16-18 KJV**
*16 But this is that which was spoken by the prophet Joel;*
*17 And it shall come to pass in the last days, saith God, I will pour out of my Spirit upon all flesh: and your sons and your daughters shall prophesy, and your young men shall see visions, and your old men shall dream dreams:*
*18 And on my servants and on my handmaidens I will pour out in those days of my Spirit; and they shall prophesy:*

**Acts 2:39** *For the promise is unto you, and to your children, and to all that are afar off, even as many as the Lord our God shall call. KJV*

**63. Read the following passage and note by underlining the blessings of the Holy Spirit Rom. 8:1-28 KJV**

*1 There is therefore now no condemnation to them which are in Christ Jesus, who walk not after the flesh, but after the Spirit.*
*2 For the law of the Spirit of life in Christ Jesus hath made me free from the law of sin and death.*
*3 For what the law could not do, in that it was weak through the flesh, God sending his own Son in the likeness of sinful flesh, and for sin, condemned sin in the flesh:*
*4 That the righteousness of the law might be fulfilled in us, who walk not after the flesh, but after the Spirit.*
*5 For they that are after the flesh do mind the things of the flesh; but they that are after the Spirit the things of the Spirit.*
*6 For to be carnally minded is death; but to be spiritually minded is life and peace.*
*7 Because the carnal mind is enmity against God: for it is not subject to the law of God, neither indeed can be.*
*8 So then they that are in the flesh cannot please God.*
*9 But ye are not in the flesh, but in the Spirit, if so be that the Spirit of God dwell in you. Now if any man have not the Spirit of Christ, he is none of his.*
*10 And if Christ be in you, the body is dead because of sin; but the Spirit is life because of righteousness.*
*11 But if the Spirit of him that raised up Jesus from the dead dwell in you, he that raised up Christ from the dead shall also quicken your mortal bodies by his Spirit that dwelleth in you.*
*12 Therefore, brethren, we are debtors, not to the flesh, to live after the flesh.*
*13 For if ye live after the flesh, ye shall die: but if ye through the Spirit do mortify the deeds of the body, ye shall live.*
*14 For as many as are led by the Spirit of God, they are the sons of God.*
*15 For ye have not received the spirit of bondage again to fear; but ye have received the Spirit of adoption, whereby we cry, Abba, Father.*

*16 The Spirit itself beareth witness with our spirit, that we are the children of God:*
*17 And if children, then heirs; heirs of God, and joint-heirs with Christ; if so be that we suffer with him, that we may be also glorified together.*
*18 For I reckon that the sufferings of this present time are not worthy to be compared with the glory which shall be revealed in us.*
*19 For the earnest expectation of the creature waiteth for the manifestation of the sons of God.*
*20 For the creature was made subject to vanity, not willingly, but by reason of him who hath subjected the same in hope,*
*21 Because the creature itself also shall be delivered from the bondage of corruption into the glorious liberty of the children of God.*
*22 For we know that the whole creation groaneth and travaileth in pain together until now.*
*23 And not only they, but ourselves also, which have the firstfruits of the Spirit, even we ourselves groan within ourselves, waiting for the adoption, to wit, the redemption of our body.*
*24 For we are saved by hope: but hope that is seen is not hope: for what a man seeth, why doth he yet hope for?*
*25 But if we hope for that we see not, then do we with patience wait for it.*
*26 Likewise the Spirit also helpeth our infirmities: for we know not what we should pray for as we ought: but the Spirit itself maketh intercession for us with groanings which cannot be uttered.*
*27 And he that searcheth the hearts knoweth what is the mind of the Spirit, because he maketh intercession for the saints according to the will of God.*
*28 And we know that all things work together for good to them that love God, to them who are the called according to his purpose.*

### 64. The Holy Spirit enables for complete preaching of the gospel through signs and wonders Rom. 15:19 KJV

*19 Through mighty signs and wonders, by the power of the Spirit of God; so that from Jerusalem, and round about unto Illyricum, I have fully preached the gospel of Christ.*

**1 Cor. 2:4-5 KJV**

*4 And my speech and my preaching was not with enticing words of man's wisdom, but in demonstration of the Spirit and of power:*
*5 That your faith should not stand in the wisdom of men, but in the power of God.*

### 65. The Holy Spirit is given that we may know what things are freely given to us of God 1 Cor. 2:10-14 KJV

*10 But God hath revealed them unto us by his Spirit: for the Spirit searcheth all things, yea, the deep things of God.*
*11 For what man knoweth the things of a man, save the spirit of man which is in him? even so the things of God knoweth no man, but the Spirit of God.*
*12 Now we have received, not the spirit of the world, but the spirit which is of God; that we might know the things that are freely given to us of God.*
*13 Which things also we speak, not in the words which man's wisdom teacheth, but which the Holy Ghost teacheth; comparing spiritual things with spiritual.*
*14 But the natural man receiveth not the things of the Spirit of God: for they are foolishness unto him: neither can he know them, because they are spiritually discerned.*

## 66. The Holy Spirit gives us the mind of Christ 1 Cor. 2:9-16 KJV

*9 But as it is written, Eye hath not seen, nor ear heard, neither have entered into the heart of man, the things which God hath prepared for them that love him.*
*10 But God hath revealed them unto us by his Spirit: for the Spirit searcheth all things, yea, the deep things of God.*
*11 For what man knoweth the things of a man, save the spirit of man which is in him? even so the things of God knoweth no man, but the Spirit of God.*
*12 Now we have received, not the spirit of the world, but the spirit which is of God; that we might know the things that are freely given to us of God.*
*13 Which things also we speak, not in the words which man's wisdom teacheth, but which the Holy Ghost teacheth; comparing spiritual things with spiritual.*
*14 But the natural man receiveth not the things of the Spirit of God: for they are foolishness unto him: neither can he know them, because they are spiritually discerned.*
*15 But he that is spiritual judgeth all things, yet he himself is judged of no man.*
*16 For who hath known the mind of the Lord, that he may instruct him? But we have the mind of Christ.*

## 67. The Holy Spirit enables you to confess that Jesus is the Lord 1 Cor. 12:3 KJV

*3 Wherefore I give you to understand, that no man speaking by the Spirit of God calleth Jesus accursed: and that no man can say that Jesus is the Lord, but by the Holy Ghost.*

## 68. The Holy Spirit has gifts for each individual believer 1 Cor. 12:4-11 KJV

*4 Now there are diversities of gifts, but the same Spirit.*
*5 And there are differences of administrations, but the same Lord.*
*6 And there are diversities of operations, but it is the same God which worketh all in all.*
*7 But the manifestation of the Spirit is given to every man to profit withal.*

1. **Every man** SC each or every

    a. This Greek word is used in the King James Version several different ways: any, both, each (one), every (man, one, woman), particularly

*8 For to one is given by the Spirit the word of wisdom; to another the word of knowledge by the same Spirit;*
*9 To another faith by the same Spirit; to another the gifts of healing by the same Spirit;*
*10 To another the working of miracles; to another prophecy; to another discerning of spirits; to another divers kinds of tongues; to another the interpretation of tongues:*
*11 But all these worketh that one and the selfsame Spirit, dividing to every man severally as he will.*

## 69. The Holy Spirit baptizes us into one body 1 Cor. 12:13 KJV

*13 For by one Spirit are we all baptized into one body, whether we be Jews or Gentiles, whether we be bond or free; and have been all made to drink into one Spirit.*

a. **Baptized** SC NT: to immerse, submerge; to make overwhelmed (i.e. fully wet)

1. SC NT: to overwhelm, i.e. cover wholly with a fluid; (by implication) to stain (as with dye)

**70. The Holy Spirit is a seal, a deposit and guarantee of the fulfillment of His promise 2 Cor. 1:22 AMP**

*22[He has also appropriated and acknowledged us as His by] putting His seal upon us and giving us His [Holy] Spirit in our hearts as the security deposit and guarantee [of the fulfillment of His promise].*

**2 Cor. 5:5** *Now he that hath wrought us for the selfsame thing is God, who also hath given unto us the earnest of the Spirit. KJV*

**71. The Holy Spirit writes upon our hearts that we are a letter from Christ 2 Cor. 3:1-3 AMP**

*1 ARE WE starting to commend ourselves again? Or we do not, like some [false teachers], need written credentials or letters of recommendation to you or from you, [do we]?*
*2[No] you yourselves are our letter of recommendation (our credentials), written in your hearts, to be known (perceived, recognized) and read by everybody.*
*3 You show and make obvious that you are a letter from Christ delivered by us, not written with ink but with [the] Spirit of [the] living God, not on tablets of stone but on tablets of human hearts. [Ex. 24:12; 31:18; 32:15, 16; Jer. 31:33.]*

**72. The Holy Spirit changes us from glory to glory into His image 2 Cor. 3:18 KJV**

*18 But we all, with open face beholding as in a glass the glory of the Lord, are changed into the same image from glory to glory, even as by the Spirit of the Lord.*

**73. The Holy Spirit is received by faith Gal. 3:2-5 KJV**

*2 This only would I learn of you, Received ye the Spirit by the works of the law, or by the hearing of faith?*
*3 Are ye so foolish? having begun in the Spirit, are ye now made perfect by the flesh?*
*4 Have ye suffered so many things in vain? if it be yet in vain.*
*5 He therefore that ministereth to you the Spirit, and worketh miracles among you, doeth he it by the works of the law, or by the hearing of faith?*

**Gal. 3:14** *That the blessing of Abraham might come on the Gentiles through Jesus Christ; that we might receive the promise of the Spirit through faith. KJV*

**74. The Holy Spirit declares that we are the sons of God Gal. 4:4-6 KJV**

*4 But when the fullness of the time was come, God sent forth his Son, made of a woman, made under the law,*
*5 To redeem them that were under the law, that we might receive the adoption of sons.*
*6 And because ye are sons, God hath sent forth the Spirit of his Son into your hearts, crying, Abba, Father.*

**75. The Holy Spirit is to be experienced by walking and living and in Him Gal. 5:16-25 KJV**

*16 This I say then, Walk in the Spirit, and ye shall not fulfil the lust of the flesh.*
*17 For the flesh lusteth against the Spirit, and the Spirit against the flesh: and these are contrary the one to the other: so that ye cannot do the things that ye would.*
*18 But if ye be led of the Spirit, ye are not under the law.*
*19 Now the works of the flesh are manifest, which are these; Adultery, fornication, uncleanness, lasciviousness,*
*20 Idolatry, witchcraft, hatred, variance, emulations, wrath, strife, seditions, heresies,*
*21 Envyings, murders, drunkenness, revellings, and such like: of the which I tell you before, as I have also told you in time past, that they which do such things shall not inherit the kingdom of God.*
*22 But the fruit of the Spirit is love, joy, peace, longsuffering, gentleness, goodness, faith,*
*23 Meekness, temperance: against such there is no law.*
*24 And they that are Christ's have crucified the flesh with the affections and lusts.*
*25 If we live in the Spirit, let us also walk in the Spirit.*

**76. Sowing and reaping are involved with the Holy Spirit – corruption or life everlasting Gal. 6:8-9 KJV**

*8 For he that soweth to his flesh shall of the flesh reap corruption; but he that soweth to the Spirit shall of the Spirit reap life everlasting.*
*9 And let us not be weary in well doing: for in due season we shall reap, if we faint not.*

# ACTIONS (77-89)

## INTRO:

**The actions of the Holy Spirit are activities that work as benefits to the believer. These individual experiences propel the believer in his or her walk with God. The actions of Holy Spirit are as follows:**

**77. The Holy Spirit of promise seals you Eph. 1:13 KJV**

*13 In whom ye also trusted, after that ye heard the word of truth, the gospel of your salvation: in whom also after that ye believed, ye were sealed with that Holy Spirit of promise,*

1. **Sealed** SC: to stamp (with a signet or private mark) for security or preservation (literally or figuratively); by implication, to keep secret, to attest

   a. SC NT: a signet (as fencing in or protecting from misappropriation); by implication, the stamp impressed (as a mark of privacy, or genuineness), literally or figuratively

   b. **SC NT:** to fence or enclose, i.e. (specifically) to block up (figuratively, to silence)

**78. The Holy Spirit gives us access (both Jew and Gentile) to the father Eph. 2:18 KJV**

*18 For through him we both have access by one Spirit unto the Father.*

**79. The Holy Spirit is an offensive weapon – the sword of the Spirit the word of God Eph. 6:17 KJV**

*17 And take the helmet of salvation, and the sword of the Spirit, which is the word of God:*

**80. The Holy Spirit preserves spiritual health and the welfare of the soul Phil. 1:19 KJV AMP**

*19 For I am well assured and indeed know that through your prayers and a bountiful supply of the Spirit of Jesus Christ (the Messiah) this will turn out for my preservation (for the spiritual health and welfare of my own soul) and avail toward the saving work of the Gospel.*

**81. The Holy Spirit gives instruction concerning the last days 1 Tim. 4:1 KJV**

*1 Now the Spirit speaketh expressly, that in the latter times some shall depart from the faith, giving heed to seducing spirits, and doctrines of devils;*

**82. The Spirit gives assurance by his abiding presence 1 John 3:24 KJV**

*24 And he that keepeth his commandments dwelleth in him, and he in him. And hereby we know that he abideth in us, by the Spirit which he hath given us.*

**1 John 4:13** *Hereby know we that we dwell in him, and he in us, because he hath given us of his Spirit. KJV*

**83. The Holy Spirit provides a test for revealing the spirit of antichrist Christ 1 John 4:1-3 KJV**

*1 Beloved, believe not every spirit, but try the spirits whether they are of God: because many false prophets are gone out into the world.*
*2 Hereby know ye the Spirit of God: Every spirit that confesseth that Jesus Christ is come in the flesh is of God:*
*3 And every spirit that confesseth not that Jesus Christ is come in the flesh is not of God: and this is that spirit of antichrist, whereof ye have heard that it should come; and even now already is it in the world.*

**84. The Holy Spirit is a witness 1 John 5:6-9 KJV**

*6 This is he that came by water and blood, even Jesus Christ; not by water only, but by water and blood. And it is the Spirit that beareth witness, because the Spirit is truth.*
*7 For there are three that bear record in heaven, the Father, the Word, and the Holy Ghost: and these three are one.*
*8 And there are three that bear witness in earth, the spirit, and the water, and the blood: and these three agree in one.*
*9 If we receive the witness of men, the witness of God is greater: for this is the witness of God which he hath testified of his Son.*

**85. The Holy Spirit says come and take the water of life Rev. 22:17 KJV**

*17 And the Spirit and the bride say, Come. And let him that heareth say, Come. And let him that is athirst come. And whosoever will, let him take the water of life freely.*

**86. The Holy Spirit brings joy to the saints Rom. 14:17 AMP**

*17 [After all] the kingdom of God is not a matter of [getting the] food and drink [one likes], but instead it is righteousness (that state which makes a person acceptable to God) and [heart] peace and joy in the Holy Spirit.*

**Acts 13:52** *And the disciples were filled with joy, and with the Holy Ghost. KJV*

**Gal 5:22-23 KJV**
*22 But the fruit of the Spirit is love, joy, peace, longsuffering, gentleness, goodness, faith,*

*23 Meekness, temperance: against such there is no law.*

**1 Thess. 1:6** *And ye became followers of us, and of the Lord, having received the word in much affliction, with joy of the Holy Ghost: KJV*

**87. The Holy Spirit can comfort. Acts 9:31 KJV**

*31 Then had the churches rest throughout all Judaea and Galilee and Samaria, and were edified; and walking in the fear of the Lord, and in the comfort of the Holy Ghost, were multiplied.*

1. **Comfort** SC NT: imploration, hortation, solace

**89. The Holy Spirit can signify what is right 1 Peter 1:11 KJV**

*11 Searching what, or what manner of time the Spirit of Christ which was in them did signify, when it testified beforehand the sufferings of Christ, and the glory that should follow.*

**Acts 15:28** *For it seemed good to the Holy Ghost, and to us, to lay upon you no greater burden than these necessary things; KJV*

a. **Signify** SC NT: to make plain (by words) clear

# MANKIND AND TREATMENT

## INTRO:

**The Holy Spirit experiences different responses from mankind. In reality He can be treated just like any other human being. There are two different sides in our response to the Holy Spirit. One is to respond in a negative way and the other is to respond positively.**

**I. The negative responses to the Holy Spirit**

**A. The Holy Spirit can be lied to. Acts 4:36-5:11 KJV**

*36 And Joses, who by the apostles was surnamed Barnabas, (which is, being interpreted, The son of consolation,) a Levite, and of the country of Cyprus,*
*37 Having land, sold it, and brought the money, and laid it at the apostles' feet.*
*5:1 But a certain man named Ananias, with Sapphira his wife, sold a possession,*
*2 And kept back part of the price, his wife also being privy to it, and brought a certain part, and laid it at the apostles' feet.*
*3 But Peter said, Ananias, why hath Satan filled thine heart to lie to the Holy Ghost, and to keep back part of the price of the land?*
*4 Whiles it remained, was it not thine own? and after it was sold, was it not in thine own power? why hast thou conceived this thing in thine heart? thou hast not lied unto men, but unto God.*
*5 And Ananias hearing these words fell down, and gave up the ghost: and great fear came on all them that heard these things.*
*6 And the young men arose, wound him up, and carried him out, and buried him.*
*7 And it was about the space of three hours after, when his wife, not knowing what was done, came in.*
*8 And Peter answered unto her, Tell me whether ye sold the land for so much? And she said, Yea, for so much.*
*9 Then Peter said unto her, How is it that ye have agreed together to tempt the Spirit of the Lord? behold, the feet of them which have buried thy husband are at the door, and shall carry thee out.*
*10 Then fell she down straightway at his feet, and yielded up the ghost: and the young men came in, and found her dead, and, carrying her forth, buried her by her husband.*
*11 And great fear came upon all the church, and upon as many as heard these things.*

**B. The Holy Spirit can be tested Acts 5:9 KJV**

*9 Then Peter said unto her, How is it that ye have agreed together to tempt the Spirit of the Lord? behold, the feet of them which have buried thy husband are at the door, and shall carry thee out.*

1. **Tempted** SC NT: to test (objectively), i.e. endeavor, scrutinize, entice, discipline

   a. SC NT: (through the idea of piercing); a test, i.e. attempt, experience

2. **Moses had a controversy with Israel Ex. 17:1-3 KJV**

   *1 And all the congregation of the children of Israel journeyed from the wilderness of Sin, after their journeys, according to the commandment of the LORD, and pitched in Rephidim: and there was no water for the people to drink.*
   *2 Wherefore the people did chide with Moses, and said, Give us water that we may drink. And Moses said unto them, Why chide ye with me? Wherefore do ye tempt the LORD?*
   *3 And the people thirsted there for water; and the people murmured against Moses, and said, Wherefore is this that thou hast brought us up out of Egypt, to kill us and our children and our cattle with thirst?*

   a. **Chide** SC OT: properly, to toss, i.e. grapple; mostly figuratively, to wrangle, i.e. hold a controversy; (by implication) to defend

   **Deut. 6:16-17 KJV**
   *16 Ye shall not tempt the LORD your God, as ye tempted him in Massah.*
   *17 Ye shall diligently keep the commandments of the LORD your God, and his testimonies, and his statutes, which he hath commanded thee.*

   **Ex. 17:5-7 KJV**
   *5 And the LORD said unto Moses, Go on before the people, and take with thee of the elders of Israel; and thy rod, wherewith thou smotest the river, take in thine hand, and go.*
   *6 Behold, I will stand before thee there upon the rock in Horeb; and thou shalt smite the rock, and there shall come water out of it, that the people may drink. And Moses did so in the sight of the elders of Israel.*
   *7 And he called the name of the place Massah, and Meribah, because of the chiding of the children of Israel, and because they tempted the LORD, saying, Is the LORD among us, or not?*

C. **The Holy Spirit experiences grief Eph. 4:29-30 KJV**

*29 Let no corrupt communication proceed out of your mouth, but that which is good to the use of edifying, that it may minister grace unto the hearers.*
*30 And grieve not the Holy Spirit of God, whereby ye are sealed unto the day of redemption.*

**Eph. 4:30-32 AMP**
*30 And do not grieve the Holy Spirit of God [do not offend or vex or sadden Him], by Whom you were sealed (marked, branded as God's own, secured) for the day of redemption (of final deliverance through Christ from evil and the consequences of sin).*

*31 Let all bitterness and indignation and wrath (passion, rage, bad temper) and resentment (anger, animosity) and quarreling (brawling, clamor, contention) and slander (evil-speaking, abusive or blasphemous language) be banished from you, with all malice (spite, ill will, or baseness of any kind).*
*32 And become useful and helpful and kind to one another, tenderhearted (compassionate, understanding, loving-hearted), forgiving one another [readily and freely], as God in Christ forgave you.*

1. **Grieve** SC NT: to distress; reflexively or passively, to be sad

    a. SC NT: a primary word; sadness

**D. The fire of the Holy Spirit can be quenched 1 Thess. 5:16-20 KJV**

*16 Rejoice evermore.*
*17 Pray without ceasing.*
*18 In everything give thanks: for this is the will of God in Christ Jesus concerning you.*
*19 Quench not the Spirit.*
*20 Despise not prophesyings.*

1. **Quench** SC NT: to extinguish (literally or figuratively)

    *19 Do not quench (suppress or subdue) the [Holy] Spirit; AMP*

    *19 Do not extinguish the Spirit's fire; RDE*

    **Matt. 25:8** *And the foolish said unto the wise, Give us of your oil; for our lamps are gone out. KJV*

**E. The Holy Spirit can be blasphemed Matt. 12:31-32 KJV**

*31 Wherefore I say unto you, All manner of sin and blasphemy shall be forgiven unto men: but the blasphemy against the Holy Ghost shall not be forgiven unto men.*
*32 And whosoever speaketh a word against the Son of man, it shall be forgiven him: but whosoever speaketh against the Holy Ghost, it shall not be forgiven him, neither in this world, neither in the world to come.*

**Matt. 12:31-32 AMP**
*31 Therefore I tell you, every sin and blasphemy (every evil, abusive, injurious speaking, or indignity against sacred things) can be forgiven men, but blasphemy against the [Holy] Spirit shall not and cannot be forgiven.*
*32 And whoever speaks a word against the Son of Man will be forgiven, but whoever speaks against the Spirit, the Holy one, will not be forgiven, either in this world and age or in the world and age to come.*

1. **Blaspheme** SC NT: vilification (especially against God)

2. **American Heritage Dictionary – vilification** – to make vicious and defamatory statements about

## F. The Holy Spirit can be insulted Heb. 10:29 KJV

*29 Of how much sorer punishment, suppose ye, shall he be thought worthy, who hath trodden underfoot the Son of God, and hath counted the blood of the covenant, wherewith he was sanctified, an unholy thing, and hath done despite unto the Spirit of grace?*

**Heb. 10:28-29 AMP**

*28 Any person who has violated and [thus] rejected and set at naught the Law of Moses is put to death without pity or mercy on the evidence of two or three witnesses. [Deut. 17:2-6.]*

*29 How much worse (sterner and heavier) punishment do you suppose he will be judged to deserve who has spurned and [thus] trampled underfoot the Son of God, and who has considered the covenant blood by which he was consecrated common and unhallowed, thus profaning it and insulting and outraging the [Holy] Spirit [Who imparts] grace (the unmerited favor and blessing of God)? [Ex. 24:8.]*

1. **Despite** SC NT: to insult

## G. The Holy Spirit can be resisted Acts 7:47-51 KJV

*47 But Solomon built him an house.*
*48 Howbeit the most High dwelleth not in temples made with hands; as saith the prophet,*
*49 Heaven is my throne, and earth is my footstool: what house will ye build me? saith the Lord: or what is the place of my rest?*
*50 Hath not my hand made all these things?*
*51 Ye stiffnecked and uncircumcised in heart and ears, ye do always resist the Holy Ghost: as your fathers did, so do ye.*

1. **Resist** SC NT: to oppose

   a. SC NT: opposite, i.e. instead or because of (rarely in addition to)

## H. The Holy Spirit can be vexed Isa. 63:7-10 KJV

*7 I will mention the loving kindnesses of the LORD, and the praises of the LORD, according to all that the LORD hath bestowed on us, and the great goodness toward the house of Israel, which he hath bestowed on them according to his mercies, and according to the multitude of his lovingkindnesses.*
*8 For he said, Surely they are my people, children that will not lie: so he was their Saviour.*
*9 In all their affliction he was afflicted, and the angel of his presence saved them: in his love and in his pity he redeemed them; and he bare them, and carried them all the days of old.*
*10 But they rebelled, and vexed his Holy Spirit: therefore he was turned to be their enemy, and he fought against them.*

1. **Vexed** SC OT: to carve, i.e. fabricate or fashion; hence (in a bad sense) to worry, pain or anger

**Gen. 6:6** *And it repented the LORD that he had made man on the earth, and it grieved him at his heart. KJV*

**Ps. 78:40** *How oft did they provoke him in the wilderness, and grieve him in the desert! KJV*

## I. The Holy Spirit strives - to quarrel, contend, to be in conflict with humanity Gen. 6:3 KJV

*3 And the LORD said, My spirit shall not always strive with man, for that he also is flesh: yet his days shall be an hundred and twenty years.*

1. **Strive** SC OT: to rule; by implication to judge (as umpire); also to strive (as at law)

**Ps. 106:1-48 KJV**

*1 Praise ye the LORD. O give thanks unto the LORD; for he is good: for his mercy endureth forever.*
*2 Who can utter the mighty acts of the LORD? Who can shew forth all his praise?*
*3 Blessed are they that keep judgment, and he that doeth righteousness at all times.*
*4 Remember me, O LORD, with the favor that thou bearest unto thy people: O visit me with thy salvation;*
*5 That I may see the good of thy chosen, that I may rejoice in the gladness of thy nation, that I may glory with thine inheritance.*
*6 We have sinned with our fathers, we have committed iniquity, we have done wickedly.*
*7 Our fathers understood not thy wonders in Egypt; they remembered not the multitude of thy mercies; but provoked him at the sea, even at the Red sea.*
*8 Nevertheless he saved them for his name's sake, that he might make his mighty power to be known.*
*9 He rebuked the Red sea also, and it was dried up: so he led them through the depths, as through the wilderness.*
*10 And he saved them from the hand of him that hated them, and redeemed them from the hand of the enemy.*
*11 And the waters covered their enemies: there was not one of them left.*
*12 Then believed they his words; they sang his praise.*
*13 They soon forgat his works; they waited not for his counsel:*
*14 But lusted exceedingly in the wilderness, and tempted God in the desert.*
*15 And he gave them their request; but sent leanness into their soul.*
*16 They envied Moses also in the camp, and Aaron the saint of the LORD.*
*17 The earth opened and swallowed up Dathan, and covered the company of Abiram.*
*18 And a fire was kindled in their company; the flame burned up the wicked.*
*19 They made a calf in Horeb, and worshipped the molten image.*
*20 Thus they changed their glory into the similitude of an ox that eateth grass.*
*21 They forgat God their saviour, which had done great things in Egypt;*
*22 Wondrous works in the land of Ham, and terrible things by the Red sea.*
*23 Therefore he said that he would destroy them, had not Moses his chosen stood before him in the breach, to turn away his wrath, lest he should destroy them.*
*24 Yea, they despised the pleasant land, they believed not his word:*
*25 But murmured in their tents, and hearkened not unto the voice of the LORD.*
*26 Therefore he lifted up his hand against them, to overthrow them in the wilderness:*
*27 To overthrow their seed also among the nations, and to scatter them in the lands.*
*28 They joined themselves also unto Baal-peor, and ate the sacrifices of the dead.*
*29 Thus they provoked him to anger with their inventions: and the plague break in upon them.*
*30 Then stood up Phinehas, and executed judgment: and so the plague was stayed.*

*31 And that was counted unto him for righteousness unto all generations for evermore.*
*32 They angered him also at the waters of strife, so that it went ill with Moses for their sakes:*
*33 Because they provoked his spirit, so that he spake unadvisedly with his lips.*
*34 They did not destroy the nations, concerning whom the LORD commanded them:*
*35 But were mingled among the heathen, and learned their works.*
*36 And they served their idols: which were a snare unto them.*
*37 Yea, they sacrificed their sons and their daughters unto devils,*
*38 And shed innocent blood, even the blood of their sons and of their daughters, whom they sacrificed unto the idols of Canaan: and the land was polluted with blood.*
*39 Thus were they defiled with their own works, and went a whoring with their own inventions.*
*40 Therefore was the wrath of the LORD kindled against his people, insomuch that he abhorred his own inheritance.*
*41 And he gave them into the hand of the heathen; and they that hated them ruled over them.*
*42 Their enemies also oppressed them, and they were brought into subjection under their hand.*
*43 Many times did he deliver them; but they provoked him with their counsel, and were brought low for their iniquity.*
*44 Nevertheless he regarded their affliction, when he heard their cry:*
*45 And he remembered for them his covenant, and repented according to the multitude of his mercies.*
*46 He made them also to be pitied of all those that carried them captives.*
*47 Save us, O LORD our God, and gather us from among the heathen, to give thanks unto thy holy name, and to triumph in thy praise.*
*48 Blessed be the Lord God of Israel from everlasting to everlasting: and let all the people say, Amen. Praise ye the LORD.*

## II. We can choose to have positive responses to the Holy Spirit

### A. An attitude of love unto the Spirit Rom. 15:30 KJV

*30 Now I beseech you, brethren, for the Lord Jesus Christ's sake, and for the love of the Spirit, that ye strive together with me in your prayers to God for me;*

### B. An attitude of obedience to his voice Deut. 30:2 KJV

*2 And shalt return unto the LORD thy God, and shalt obey his voice according to all that I command thee this day, thou and thy children, with all thine heart, and with all thy soul;*

**1 Tim. 4:1** *Now the Spirit speaketh expressly, that in the latter times some shall depart from the faith, giving heed to seducing spirits, and doctrines of devils; KJV*

1. **Speaketh** SC NT: out-spokenly, i.e. distinctly

### C. An attitude of fellowship, sharing, participating with him Phil. 2:1 KJV

*1 If there be therefore any consolation in Christ, if any comfort of love, if any fellowship of the Spirit, if any bowels and mercies,*

1. **Fellowship** SC NT: partnership, i.e. (literally) participation, or (social) intercourse, or (pecuniary) benefaction: a sharer, i.e. associate

**D. An attitude of fear or reverence of the Holy Spirit Acts 5:1-11 KJV**

*1 But a certain man named Ananias, with Sapphira his wife, sold a possession,*
*2 And kept back part of the price, his wife also being privy to it, and brought a certain part, and laid it at the apostles' feet.*
*3 But Peter said, Ananias, why hath Satan filled thine heart to lie to the Holy Ghost, and to keep back part of the price of the land?*
*4 Whiles it remained, was it not thine own? and after it was sold, was it not in thine own power? why hast thou conceived this thing in thine heart? thou hast not lied unto men, but unto God.*
*5 And Ananias hearing these words fell down, and gave up the ghost: and great fear came on all them that heard these things.*
*6 And the young men arose, wound him up, and carried him out, and buried him.*
*7 And it was about the space of three hours after, when his wife, not knowing what was done, came in.*
*8 And Peter answered unto her, Tell me whether ye sold the land for so much? And she said, Yea, for so much.*
*9 Then Peter said unto her, How is it that ye have agreed together to tempt the Spirit of the Lord? behold, the feet of them which have buried thy husband are at the door, and shall carry thee out.*
*10 Then fell she down straightway at his feet, and yielded up the ghost: and the young men came in, and found her dead, and, carrying her forth, buried her by her husband.*
*11 And great fear came upon all the church, and upon as many as heard these things.*

**E. An attitude of thankfulness for:**

1. **Your salvation** **Eph. 2:8 KJV**

*8 For by grace are ye saved through faith; and that not of yourselves: it is the gift of God:*

2. **Your personal call** **Acts 13:1-4, Eph. 3:7-8 KJV**

**Acts 13:1-4 KJV**

*1 Now there were in the church that was at Antioch certain prophets and teachers; as Barnabas, and Simeon that was called Niger, and Lucius of Cyrene, and Manaen, which had been brought up with Herod the tetrarch, and Saul.*
*2 As they ministered to the Lord, and fasted, the Holy Ghost said, Separate me Barnabas and Saul for the work where unto I have called them.*
*3 And when they had fasted and prayed, and laid their hands on them, they sent them away.*
*4 So they, being sent forth by the Holy Ghost, departed unto Seleucia; and from thence they sailed to Cyprus.*

**Eph. 3:7-8 KJV**

*7 Whereof I was made a minister, according to the gift of the grace of God given unto me by the effectual working of his power.*
*8 Unto me, who am less than the least of all saints, is this grace given, that I should preach among the Gentiles the unsearchable riches of Christ;*

**3. The prophetic words that came to you through others by the Holy Spirit 1 Tim. 4:14 KJV**

*14 Neglect not the gift that is in thee, which was given thee by prophecy, with the laying on of the hands of the presbytery.*

**III. Make your own list of the ways that the Holy Spirit has ministered to you! Include in your list those things that were difficult. If there is still pain and unfinished business that is in your life look to the Word for your answers. Consider these scriptures:**

**Rom. 8:27-28 AMP**
*27 And He Who searches the hearts of men knows what is in the mind of the [Holy] Spirit [what His intent is], because the Spirit intercedes and pleads [before God] in behalf of the saints according to and in harmony with God's will. [Ps. 139:1, 2.]*
*28 We are assured and know that [God being a partner in their labor] all things work together and are [fitting into a plan] for good to and for those who love God and are called according to [His] design and purpose.*

**Ps. 119:133** *Establish my steps and direct them by [means of] Your word; let not any iniquity have dominion over me. AMP*

**Matt. 6:12-15 KJV**
*12 And forgive us our debts, as we forgive our debtors.*
*13 And lead us not into temptation, but deliver us from evil: For thine is the kingdom, and the power, and the glory, forever. Amen.*
*14 For if ye forgive men their trespasses, your heavenly Father will also forgive you:*
*15 But if ye forgive not men their trespasses, neither will your Father forgive your trespasses.*

**Eph. 4:30-32 KJV**
*30 And grieve not the holy Spirit of God, whereby ye are sealed unto the day of redemption.*
*31 Let all bitterness, and wrath, and anger, and clamour, and evil speaking, be put away from you, with all malice:*
*32 And be ye kind one to another, tenderhearted, forgiving one another, even as God for Christ's sake hath forgiven you.*

**Heb. 12:15** *Looking diligently lest any man fail of the grace of God; lest any root of bitterness springing up trouble you, and thereby many be defiled; KJV*

**Phil 4:6-9 KJV**
*6 Be careful for nothing; but in every thing by prayer and supplication with thanksgiving let your requests be made known unto God.*
*7 And the peace of God, which passeth all understanding, shall keep your hearts and minds through Christ Jesus.*

8 *Finally, brethren, whatsoever things are true, whatsoever things are honest, whatsoever things are just, whatsoever things are pure, whatsoever things are lovely, whatsoever things are of good report; if there be any virtue, and if there be any praise, think on these things.*
9 *Those things, which ye have both learned, and received, and heard, and seen in me, do: and the God of peace shall be with you.*

# DEITY

## INTRO:

**The American Heritage Dictionary** defines deity as the divine character or nature of the Supreme Being. A god or goddess. The essential nature or condition of being a god; divinity.

**The New World Dictionary** defines deity as the state of being a god; divine nature, godhood

**The attributes of the Holy Spirit** reveal his character, service, and functions

**I. There are divine attributes ascribed to the Holy Spirit that both the Father and Son possess**

**A. The Holy Spirit is omniscient (all-knowing)**

**1. He will teach you all things John 14:26 KJV**

*26 But the Comforter, which is the Holy Ghost, whom the Father will send in my name, he shall teach you all things, and bring all things to your remembrance, whatsoever I have said unto you.*

**2. He will guide you into all truth John 16:12-13 KJV**

*12 I have yet many things to say unto you, but ye cannot bear them now.*
*13 Howbeit when he, the Spirit of truth, is come, he will guide you into all truth: for he shall not speak of himself; but whatsoever he shall hear, that shall he speak: and he will shew you things to come.*

**3. He will search and investigate the deep things of God I Cor. 2:10 KJV**

*10 But God hath revealed them unto us by his Spirit: for the Spirit searcheth all things, yea, the deep things of God. KJV*

**a. Searcheth** SC NT: (through the idea of inquiry); to seek, i.e. (figuratively) to investigate

**b. Deep** SC NT: profundity, i.e. (by implication) extent; (figuratively) mystery

4. **The Holy Spirit knows how and what to pray, concerning the will of God Rom. 8:26-27 KJV**

*26 Likewise the Spirit also helpeth our infirmities: for we know not what we should pray for as we ought: but the Spirit itself maketh intercession for us with groanings which cannot be uttered.*
*27 And he that searcheth the hearts knoweth what is the mind of the Spirit, because he maketh intercession for the saints according to the will of God.*

**B. The Holy Spirit is omnipotent (all powerful)**

1. **The virgin birth Christ Luke 1:35 KJV**

*35 And the angel answered and said unto her, The Holy Ghost shall come upon thee, and the power of the Highest shall overshadow thee: therefore also that holy thing which shall be born of thee shall be called the Son of God.*

2. **Signs and wonders Rom. 15:19 KJV**

*19 Through mighty signs and wonders, by the power of the Spirit of God; so that from Jerusalem, and round about unto Illyricum, I have fully preached the gospel of Christ.*

3. **He has power over human life. Acts 5:3-5 KJV**

*3 But Peter said, Ananias, why hath Satan filled thine heart to lie to the Holy Ghost, and to keep back part of the price of the land?*
*4 Whiles it remained, was it not thine own? and after it was sold, was it not in thine own power? why hast thou conceived this thing in thine heart? thou hast not lied unto men, but unto God.*
*5 And Ananias hearing these words fell down, and gave up the ghost: and great fear came on all them that heard these things.*

4. **He was involved in the creation Gen. 1:1-2 KJV**

*1 In the beginning God created the heaven and the earth.*
*2 And the earth was without form, and void; and darkness was upon the face of the deep. And the Spirit of God moved upon the face of the waters.*

a. **Moved** SC OT: to brood; by implication, to be relaxed

**C. The Holy Spirit is eternal Heb. 9:14 KJV**

*14 How much more shall the blood of Christ, who through the eternal Spirit offered himself without spot to God, purge your conscience from dead works to serve the living God?*

**D. The Holy Spirit is called God Acts 5:3-4 KJV**

*3 But Peter said, Ananias, why hath Satan filled thine heart to lie to the Holy Ghost, and to keep back part of the price of the land?*

*4 Whiles it remained, was it not thine own? and after it was sold, was it not in thine own power? why hast thou conceived this thing in thine heart? thou hast not lied unto men, but unto God.*

**1 Cor. 3:16** *Know ye not that ye are the temple of God, and that the Spirit of God dwelleth in you? KJV*

**1 Cor. 12:4-6 KJV**

*4 Now there are diversities of gifts, but the same Spirit.*
*5 And there are differences of administrations, but the same Lord.*
*6 And there are diversities of operations, but it is the same God which worketh all in all.*

## E. The Holy Spirit is omnipresent (present everywhere) Ps. 139:7-10 KJV

*7 Whither shall I go from thy spirit? or whither shall I flee from thy presence?*
*8 If I ascend up into heaven, thou art there: if I make my bed in hell, behold, thou art there.*
*9 If I take the wings of the morning, and dwell in the uttermost parts of the sea;*
*10 Even there shall thy hand lead me, and thy right hand shall hold me.*

## F. The Holy Spirit is the Spirit of Life Rom. 8:1-2 KJV

*1 There is therefore now no condemnation to them which are in Christ Jesus, who walk not after the flesh, but after the Spirit.*

*2 For the law of the Spirit of life in Christ Jesus hath made me free from the law of sin and death.*

**Rom. 8:10** *And if Christ be in you, the body is dead because of sin; but the Spirit is life because of righteousness. KJV*

**Gal. 6:8** *For he that soweth to his flesh shall of the flesh reap corruption; but he that soweth to the Spirit shall of the Spirit reap life everlasting. KJV*

**Rev. 11:11** *And after three days and an half the Spirit of life from God entered into them, and they stood upon their feet; and great fear fell upon them which saw them. KJV*

## G. The Holy Spirit is mentioned with the Father and Son Matt. 28:18-20 KJV

*18 And Jesus came and spake unto them, saying, All power is given unto me in heaven and in earth.*

*19 Go ye therefore, and teach all nations, baptizing them in the name of the Father, and of the Son, and of the Holy Ghost:*

*20 Teaching them to observe all things whatsoever I have commanded you: and, lo, I am with you alway, even unto the end of the world. Amen.*

## H. The Holy Spirit is the spirit of glory and of God 1 Peter 4:14 KJV

*14 If ye be reproached for the name of Christ, happy are ye; for the spirit of glory and of God resteth upon you: on their part he is evil spoken of, but on your part he is glorified.*

**I. The Holy Spirit was involved in the creation of mankind Gen. 1:26 KJV**

*26 And God said, Let us make man in our image, after our likeness: and let them have dominion over the fish of the sea, and over the fowl of the air, and over the cattle, and over all the earth, and over every creeping thing that creepeth upon the earth.*

**a. God** SC OT: gods in the ordinary sense; but specifically used (in the plural thus, especially with the article) of the supreme God

**1.** SC OT: a deity or the Deity

**Job 33:4** *The Spirit of God hath made me, and the breath of the Almighty hath given me life. KJV*

**J. The Holy Spirit distributes the grace of God within the body of Christ 1 Cor. 12:4-7 KJV**

*4 Now there are diversities of gifts, but the same Spirit.*
*5 And there are differences of administrations, but the same Lord.*
*6 And there are diversities of operations, but it is the same God which worketh all in all.*
*7 But the manifestation of the Spirit is given to every man to profit withal.*

**John 1:16-17 AMP**
*16 For out of His fullness (abundance) we have all received [all had a share and we were all supplied with] one grace after another and spiritual blessing upon spiritual blessing and even favor upon favor and gift [heaped] upon gift.*
*17 For while the Law was given through Moses, grace (unearned, undeserved favor and spiritual blessing) and truth came through Jesus Christ. [Ex 20:1.]*

**Rom. 12:6** *Having then gifts differing according to the grace that is given to us, whether prophecy, let us prophesy according to the proportion of faith; KJV*

**2 Cor. 9:8** *And God is able to make all grace abound toward you; that ye, always having all sufficiency in all things, may abound to every good work: KJV*

**K. The Holy Spirit is the author of the new birth John 3:5-8 KJV**

*5 Jesus answered, Verily, verily, I say unto thee, Except a man be born of water and of the Spirit, he cannot enter into the kingdom of God.*
*6 That which is born of the flesh is flesh; and that which is born of the Spirit is spirit.*
*7 Marvel not that I said unto thee, Ye must be born again.*
*8 The wind bloweth where it listeth, and thou hearest the sound thereof, but canst not tell whence it cometh, and whither it goeth: so is every one that is born of the Spirit.*

## L. The Holy Spirit has the power over death 1 Pet. 3:18 KJV

*18 For Christ also hath once suffered for sins, the just for the unjust, that he might bring us to God, being put to death in the flesh, but quickened by the Spirit:*

## M. The scripture is given by the inspiration of God 2 Tim. 3:16-17 KJV

*16 All scripture is given by inspiration of God, and is profitable for doctrine, for reproof, for correction, for instruction in righteousness:*
*17 That the man of God may be perfect, thoroughly furnished unto all good works.*

1. **Inspiration** SC NT: divinely breathed in

2. **SC NT:** a deity, the supreme Divinity

# OLD TESTAMENT TITLES & DESCRIPTIONS

## INTRO:

**Each title given to the Holy Spirit reveals a side of God that ministers to the believer**

**I. There are 15 different titles and descriptions in the Old Testament**

**A. He is called the Spirit of God Gen. 1:2 (KJV)**

*2 And the earth was without form, and void; and darkness was upon the face of the deep. And the Spirit of God moved upon the face of the waters.*

1. **Spirit** SC OT: wind; by resemblance breath, i.e. a sensible (or even violent) exhalation; figuratively, life, anger, unsubstantiality; by extension, a region of the sky;_by resemblance spirit, but only of a rational being (including its expression and functions)

2. **God** SC OT: gods in the ordinary sense; but specifically used (in the plural thus, especially with the article) of the supreme God

**Job 33:4** *The Spirit of God hath made me, and the breath of the Almighty hath given me life.* (KJV)

**Matt. 3:16** *And Jesus, when he was baptized, went up straightway out of the water: and, lo, the heavens were opened unto him, and he saw the Spirit of God descending like a dove, and lighting upon him:* (KJV)

**Eph. 4:30** *And grieve not the Holy Spirit of God, whereby ye are sealed unto the day of redemption.* KJV

**1 Cor. 3:16** *Know ye not that ye are the temple of God, and that the Spirit of God dwelleth in you?* KJV

**B. The Breath of the Almighty Job 33:8 KJV**

*8 The Spirit of God hath made me, and the breath of the Almighty hath given me life.*

**Job 32:8** *But there is a spirit in man: and the inspiration of the Almighty giveth them understanding. KJV*

1. **Breath** SC OT: a puff, i.e. wind, angry or vital breath, divine inspiration, intellect

## C. The Free Spirit Ps. 51:12 KJV

*12 Restore unto me the joy of thy salvation; and uphold me with thy free spirit.*

1. **Free** SC OT: voluntary, i.e. generous; hence, magnanimous; as noun, a grandee

2. SC OT: a primitive root; to impel; hence, to volunteer (as a soldier), to present spontaneously

## D. The Spirit of Judgment Isa. 4:4 KJV

*4 When the Lord shall have washed away the filth of the daughters of Zion, and shall have purged the blood of Jerusalem from the midst thereof by the spirit of judgment, and by the spirit of burning.*

1. **Judgment** SC OT: properly, a verdict (favorable or unfavorable) pronounced judicially, especially a sentence or formal decree (human or [participant's] divine law, individual or collective), including the act, the place, the suit, the crime, and the penalty; abstractly, justice, including a participant's right or privilege (statutory or customary), or even a style:

   a. SC OT: to judge, i.e. pronounce sentence (for or against); by implication, to vindicate or punish; by extension, to govern; passively, to litigate (literally or figuratively):

2. **Judgment Example - Ananias & Sapphira Acts 5:1-10 (KJV)**

*1 But a certain man named Ananias, with Sapphira his wife, sold a possession,*
*2 And kept back part of the price, his wife also being privy to it, and brought a certain part, and laid it at the apostles' feet.*
*3 But Peter said, Ananias, why hath Satan filled thine heart to lie to the Holy Ghost, and to keep back part of the price of the land?*
*4 Whiles it remained, was it not thine own? and after it was sold, was it not in thine own power? why hast thou conceived this thing in thine heart? thou hast not lied unto men, but unto God.*
*5 And Ananias hearing these words fell down, and gave up the ghost: and great fear came on all them that heard these things.*
*6 And the young men arose, wound him up, and carried him out, and buried him.*
*7 And it was about the space of three hours after, when his wife, not knowing what was done, came in.*
*8 And Peter answered unto her, Tell me whether ye sold the land for so much? And she said, Yea, for so much.*
*9 Then Peter said unto her, How is it that ye have agreed together to tempt the Spirit of the Lord? behold, the feet of them which have buried thy husband are at the door, and shall carry thee out.*
*10 Then fell she down straightway at his feet, and yielded up the ghost: and the young men came in, and found her dead, and, carrying her forth, buried her by her husband.*

## E. The Spirit of Burning Isa. 4:4 KJV

*4 When the Lord shall have washed away the filth of the daughters of Zion, and shall have purged the blood of Jerusalem from the midst thereof by the spirit of judgment, and by the spirit of burning.*

1. **Burning** SC OT: to kindle, i.e. consume (by fire or by eating)

2. **We are to be baptized with the Holy Ghost and fire. Matt. 3:11 KJV**

   *11 I indeed baptize you with water unto repentance: but he that cometh after me is mightier than I, whose shoes I am not worthy to bear: he shall baptize you with the Holy Ghost, and with fire:*

   **Acts 2:3** *And there appeared unto them cloven tongues like as of fire, and it sat upon each of them. KJV*

3. **Fire is to burn away the chaff of wheat or dross of the metal. Matt. 3:12 NAS**

   *12 "And His winnowing fork is in His hand, and He will thoroughly clear His threshing floor; and He will gather His wheat into the barn, but He will burn up the chaff with unquenchable fire."*

   **Mal. 3:1-3 (TLB)**
   *1 "Listen: I will send my messenger before me to prepare the way. And then the One you are looking for will come suddenly to his Temple-- the Messenger of God's promises, to bring you great joy. Yes, he is surely coming," says the Lord Almighty.*
   *2 "But who can live when he appears? Who can endure his coming? For he is like a blazing fire refining precious metal, and he can bleach the dirtiest garments!*
   *3 Like a refiner of silver he will sit and closely watch as the dross is burned away. He willpurify the Levites, the ministers of God, refining them like gold or silver, so that they will do their work for God with pure hearts.*

4. **The false prophet is to be given to fire Matt. 7:15-20 KJV**

   *15 Beware of false prophets, which come to you in sheep's clothing, but inwardly they are ravening wolves.*
   *16 Ye shall know them by their fruits. Do men gather grapes of thorns, or figs of thistles?*
   *17 Even so every good tree bringeth forth good fruit; but a corrupt tree bringeth forth evil fruit.*
   *18 A good tree cannot bring forth evil fruit, neither can a corrupt tree bring forth good fruit.*
   *19 Every tree that bringeth not forth good fruit is hewn down, and cast into the fire.*
   *20 Wherefore by their fruits ye shall know them.*

   **1 Cor. 3:13** *Every man's work shall be made manifest: for the day shall declare it, because it shall be revealed by fire; and the fire shall try every man's work of what sort it is. KJV*

   **Heb. 12:29** *For our God is a consuming fire. KJV*

   **Deut. 4:24** *For the LORD thy God is a consuming fire, even a jealous God. KJV*

**Rev. 19:20** *And the beast was taken, and with him the false prophet that wrought miracles before him, with which he deceived them that had received the mark of the beast, and them that worshipped his image. These both were cast alive into a lake of fire burning with brimstone. KJV*

**Rev. 20:10** *And the devil that deceived them was cast into the lake of fire and brimstone, where the beast and the false prophet are, and shall be tormented day and night forever and ever. KJV*

## F. The Spirit of Grace and Supplications Zech. 12:10 KJV

*10 And I will pour upon the house of David, and upon the inhabitants of Jerusalem, the spirit of grace and of supplications: and they shall look upon me whom they have pierced, and they shall mourn for him, as one mourneth for his only son, and shall be in bitterness for him, as one that is in bitterness for his firstborn.*

1. **Grace** SC OT: graciousness, i.e. subjective (kindness, favor) or objective (beauty)

   a. SC OT: properly, to bend or stoop in kindness to an inferior; to favor, bestow; causatively to implore (i.e. move to favor by petition)

2. **Supplications** SC OT: earnest prayer

**Heb. 10:29** *Of how much sorer punishment, suppose ye, shall he be thought worthy, who hath trodden underfoot the Son of God, and hath counted the blood of the covenant, wherewith he was sanctified, an unholy thing, and hath done despite unto the Spirit of grace? KJV*

**Acts 1:14** *These all continued with one accord in prayer and supplication, with the women, and Mary the mother of Jesus, and with his brethren. KJV*

**Eph. 6:18** *Praying always with all prayer and supplication in the Spirit, and watching thereunto with all perseverance and supplication for all saints; KJV*

**Phil. 4:6** *Be careful for nothing; but in everything by prayer and supplication with thanksgiving let your requests be made known unto God. KJV*

## G. The Spirit of the Lord Isa. 11:2 KJV

*2 And the spirit of the LORD shall rest upon him, the spirit of wisdom and understanding, the spirit of counsel and might, the spirit of knowledge and of the fear of the LORD;*

1. **Lord** SC OT: (the) self-Existent or Eternal; Jehovah, Jewish national name of God

   a. SC OT: to exist, i.e. be or become, come to pass

   b. SC OT: a primitive root supposed to mean properly, to breathe; to be (in the sense of existence)

**Judg. 6:34** *But the Spirit of the LORD came upon Gideon, and he blew a trumpet; and Abi-ezer was gathered after him. KJV*

**Luke 4:18** *The Spirit of the Lord is upon me, because he hath anointed me to preach the gospel to the poor; he hath sent me to heal the brokenhearted, to preach deliverance to the captives, and recovering of sight to the blind, to set at liberty them that are bruised, KJV*

**H. The spirit of Wisdom and Understanding Isa. 11:2 KJV**

*2 And the spirit of the LORD shall rest upon him, the spirit of wisdom and understanding, the spirit of counsel and might, the spirit of knowledge and of the fear of the LORD;*

1. **Wisdom** SC OT: wisdom (in a good sense)

   a. SC OT: a primitive root, to be wise (in mind, word or act)

2. **Understanding** SC OT: understanding

   a. SC OT: a primitive root; to separate mentally (or distinguish), i.e. (generally) understand

**Eph. 1:17** *That the God of our Lord Jesus Christ, the Father of glory, may give unto you the spirit of wisdom and revelation in the knowledge of him: KJV*

**I. The Spirit of Counsel and Might Isa. 11:2 KJV**

*2 And the spirit of the LORD shall rest upon him, the spirit of wisdom and understanding, the spirit of counsel and might, the spirit of knowledge and of the fear of the LORD;*

1. **Counsel** SC OT: advice; by implication, plan; also prudence

   a. SC OT: a primitive root; to advise; reflexively, to deliberate or resolve

2. **Might** SC OT: force (literally or figuratively); by implication, valor, victory

   a. SC OT: powerful; by implication, warrior, tyrant

   b. SC OT: properly, a valiant man or warrior; generally, a person simply

   c. SC OT: to be strong; by implication, to prevail, act insolently

**J. The Spirit of Knowledge Isa. 11:2 KJV**

*2 And the spirit of the LORD shall rest upon him, the spirit of wisdom and understanding, the spirit of counsel and might, the spirit of knowledge and of the fear of the LORD;*

1. **Knowledge** SC OT: knowledge

    a. SC OT: a primitive root; to know (properly, to ascertain by seeing); used in a great variety of senses, figuratively, literally, euphemistically and inferentially (including observation, care, recognition; and causatively, instruction, designation, punishment, etc.)

**K. The Fear of the Lord Isa. 11:2 KJV**

*2 And the spirit of the LORD shall rest upon him, the spirit of wisdom and understanding, the spirit of counsel and might, the spirit of knowledge and of the fear of the LORD;*

1. **Fear** SC OT: fear (also used as infinitive); morally, reverence

**L. The Spirit of the Lord God Isa. 61:1 KJV**

*1 The Spirit of the Lord GOD is upon me; because the LORD hath anointed me to preach good tidings unto the meek; he hath sent me to bind up the brokenhearted, to proclaim liberty to the captives, and the opening of the prison to them that are bound;*

**M. Holy Spirit Ps. 51:11 KJV**

*11 Cast me not away from thy presence; and take not thy holy spirit from me.*

**Isa. 63:10-11 KJV**

*10 But they rebelled, and vexed his holy Spirit: therefore he was turned to be their enemy, and he fought against them.*
*11 Then he remembered the days of old, Moses, and his people, saying, Where is he that brought them up out of the sea with the shepherd of his flock? Where is he that put his holy Spirit within him?*

**N. A heathen king did not know what to call the Holy Spirit, but recognized His work in the life of Daniel. The king called the Holy Spirit, "the spirit of the holy gods" Dan. 4:9 KJV**

*9 O Belteshazzar, master of the magicians, because I know that the spirit of the holy gods is in thee, and no secret troubleth thee, tell me the visions of my dream that I have seen, and the interpretation thereof.*

**Dan. 4:18** *This dream I king Nebuchadnezzar have seen. Now thou, O Belteshazzar, declare the interpretation thereof, forasmuch as all the wise men of my kingdom are not able to make known unto me the interpretation: but thou art able; for the spirit of the holy gods is in thee. KJV*

**Dan. 5:11** *There is a man in thy kingdom, in whom is the spirit of the holy gods; and in the days of thy father light and understanding and wisdom, like the wisdom of the gods, was found in him; whom the king Nebuchadnezzar thy father, the king, I say, thy father, made master of the magicians, astrologers, Chaldeans, and soothsayers; KJV*

## O. The Good Spirit Neh. 9:20 KJV

*20 Thou gavest also thy good spirit to instruct them, and withheldest not thy manna from their mouth, and gavest them water for their thirst.*

**Ps. 143:10** *Teach me to do thy will; for thou art my God: thy spirit is good; lead me into the land of uprightness. KJV*

# THE OLD TESTAMENT

## INTRO:

**In the Old Testament the Holy Spirit moved upon a select few. These few consisted of Leaders of the nation of Israel, Judges, Kings, Priests, and Prophets. These individuals were equipped for a divine function that God had ordained. The majority of Israel did not personally experience the Holy Spirit but saw the results of His functioning. On the day of Pentecost, Acts chapter two, the Holy Spirit was poured out in a dimension that made it possible for every believer to be a partaker. The Lord fulfilled his promise of Joel 2:28-29 KJV.**

**Joel 2:28-29 KJV**

*28 And it shall come to pass afterward, that I will pour out my spirit upon all flesh; and your sons and your daughters shall prophesy, your old men shall dream dreams, your young men shall see visions:*

*29 And also upon the servants and upon the handmaids in those days will I pour out my spirit.*

**Acts 2:37-39 KJV**

*37 Now when they heard this, they were pricked in their heart, and said unto Peter and to the rest of the apostles, Men and brethren, what shall we do?*

*38 Then Peter said unto them, Repent, and be baptized every one of you in the name of Jesus Christ for the remission of sins, and ye shall receive the gift of the Holy Ghost.*

*39 For the promise is unto you, and to your children, and to all that are afar off, even as many as the Lord our God shall call.*

**Acts 2:14-18 KJV**

*14 But Peter, standing up with the eleven, lifted up his voice, and said unto them, Ye men of Judaea, and all ye that dwell at Jerusalem, be this known unto you, and hearken to my words:*

*15 For these are not drunken, as ye suppose, seeing it is but the third hour of the day.*

*16 But this is that which was spoken by the prophet Joel;*

*17 And it shall come to pass in the last days, saith God, I will pour out of my Spirit upon all flesh: and your sons and your daughters shall prophesy, and your young men shall see visions, and your old men shall dream dreams:*

*18 And on my servants and on my handmaidens I will pour out in those days of my Spirit; and they shall prophesy:*

**I. We will now consider the different words and ways that the Holy Spirit came upon men and women of the Old Testament**

A. **The first phrase is, "Came Upon"**

1. **The Prophets**

a. **Balaam Num. 24:2 KJV**

*2 And Balaam lifted up his eyes, and he saw Israel abiding in his tents according to their tribes; and the spirit of God came upon him.*

1. **Came Upon** SC OT: to exist, i.e. be or become, come to pass

a. SC OT: supposed to mean properly, to breathe; to be (in the sense of existence)

b. **Azariah the son Obed 2 Chr. 15:1-8 KJV**

*1 And the Spirit of God came upon Azariah the son of Oded:*
*8 And when Asa heard these words, and the prophecy of Oded the prophet, he took courage, and put away the abominable idols out of all the land of Judah and Benjamin, and out of the cities which he had taken from mount Ephraim, and renewed the altar of the LORD, that was before the porch of the LORD.*

2. **The Judges**

a. **Othniel the son of Kenaz, Caleb's younger brother Judges 3:10 KJV**

*10 And the Spirit of the LORD came upon him, and he judged Israel, and went out to war: and the LORD delivered Chushan-rishathaim king of Mesopotamia into his hand; and his hand prevailed against Chushan-rishathaim.*

b. **Gideon Judges 6:34 KJV**

*34 But the Spirit of the LORD came upon Gideon, and he blew a trumpet; and Abi-ezer was gathered after him.*

1. **Came Upon** SC OT: a primitive root; properly, wrap-around, i.e. (by implication) to put on a garment or clothe (oneself, or another), literally or figuratively

c. **Jephthah Judges 11:29 KJV**

*29 Then the Spirit of the LORD came upon Jephthah, and he passed over Gilead, and Manasseh, and passed over Mizpeh of Gilead, and from Mizpeh of Gilead he passed over unto the children of Ammon.*

d. **Samson Judges 14:19 KJV**

*19 And the Spirit of the LORD came upon him, and he went down to Ashkelon, and slew thirty men of them, and took their spoil, and gave change of garments unto them which expounded the riddle. And his anger was kindled, and he went up to his father's house.*

1. Came Upon SC OT: a primitive root; to push forward, in various senses (literal or figurative)

**3. The Kings – Saul and David**

**a. Saul 1 Sam. 10:10 KJV**

*10 And when they came thither to the hill, behold, a company of prophets met him; and the Spirit of God came upon him, and he prophesied among them.*

**1 Sam. 11:6** *And the Spirit of God came upon Saul when he heard those tidings, and his anger was kindled greatly. KJV*

**b. David 1 Sam. 16:13 KJV**

*13 Then Samuel took the horn of oil, and anointed him in the midst of his brethren: and the Spirit of the LORD came upon David from that day forward. So Samuel rose up, and went to Ramah.*

**4. A chief of the captains of the army**

**a. Amasai 1 Chr. 12:18 KJV**

*18 Then the spirit came upon Amasai, who was chief of the captains, and he said, Thine are we, David, and on thy side, thou son of Jesse: peace, peace be unto thee, and peace be to thine helpers; for thy God helpeth thee. Then David received them, and made them captains of the band.*

**5. The Priest**

**a. Zechariah the son Jehoiada the priest 2 Chr. 24:20 KJV**

*20 And the Spirit of God came upon Zechariah the son of Jehoiada the priest, which stood above the people, and said unto them, Thus saith God, Why transgress ye the commandments of the LORD, that ye cannot prosper? because ye have forsaken the LORD, he hath also forsaken you.*

**B. The second phrase is "came mightily upon"**

**1. Samson Judges 14:6 KJV**

*6 And the Spirit of the LORD came mightily upon him, and he rent him as he would have rent a kid, and he had nothing in his hand: but he told not his father or his mother what he had done.*

**Judges 15:14** *And when he came unto Lehi, the Philistines shouted against him: and the Spirit of the LORD came mightily upon him, and the cords that were upon his arms became as flax that was burnt with fire, and his bands loosed from off his hands. KJV*

a. **Came Mightily Upon** SC OT a primitive root; to push forward, in various senses (literal or figurative)

C. **The third phrase is "entered into"**

1. **Ezekiel the prophet**

**Ezek. 2:2** *And the spirit entered into me when he spake unto me, and set me upon my feet, that I heard him that spake unto me. KJV*

**Ezek. 3:24** *Then the spirit entered into me, and set me upon my feet, and spake with me, and said unto me, Go, shut thyself within thine house. KJV*

a. **Entered Into** SC OT: a primitive root; to go or come (in a wide variety of applications)

D. **The fourth phrase is a single word "move"**

1. **Samson the Judge Judges 13:24-25 KJV**

*24 And the woman bare a son, and called his name Samson: and the child grew, and the LORD blessed him.*
*25 And the Spirit of the LORD began to move him at times in the camp of Dan between Zorah and Eshtaol.*

a. **Move** SC OT: a primitive root; to tap, i.e. beat regularly; hence (generally) to impel or agitate

E. **The fifth phrase is another single word "filled" These were individuals that were filled for the purpose of equipping for service**

1. **Tabernacle of Moses Ex. 31:1-11 KJV**

*1 And the LORD spake unto Moses, saying,*
*2 See, I have called by name Bezaleel the son of Uri, the son of Hur, of the tribe of Judah:*
*3 And I have filled him with the spirit of God, in wisdom, and in understanding, and in knowledge, and in all manner of workmanship,*
*4 To devise cunning works, to work in gold, and in silver, and in brass,*
*5 And in cutting of stones, to set them, and in carving of timber, to work in all manner of workmanship.*
*6 And I, behold, I have given with him Aholiab, the son of Ahisamach, of the tribe of Dan: and in the hearts of all that are wise hearted I have put wisdom, that they may make all that I have commanded thee;*
*7 The tabernacle of the congregation, and the ark of the testimony, and the mercy seat that is thereupon, and all the furniture of the tabernacle,*
*8 And the table and his furniture, and the pure candlestick with all his furniture, and the altar of incense,*

*9 And the altar of burnt offering with all his furniture, and the laver and his foot,*

*10 And the cloths of service, and the holy garments for Aaron the priest, and the garments of his sons, to minister in the priest's office,*

*11 And the anointing oil, and sweet incense for the holy place: according to all that I have commanded thee shall they do.*

**Ex. 35:30-35 KJV**

*30 And Moses said unto the children of Israel, See, the LORD hath called by name Bezaleel the son of Uri, the son of Hur, of the tribe of Judah;*

*31 And he hath filled him with the spirit of God, in wisdom, in understanding, and in knowledge, and in all manner of workmanship;*

*32 And to devise curious works, to work in gold, and in silver, and in brass,*

*33 And in the cutting of stones, to set them, and in carving of wood, to make any manner of cunning work.*

*34 And he hath put in his heart that he may teach, both he, and Aholiab, the son of Ahisamach, of the tribe of Dan.*

*35 Them hath he filled with wisdom of heart, to work all manner of work, of the engraver, and of the cunning workman, and of the embroiderer, in blue, and in purple, in scarlet, and in fine linen, and of the weaver, even of them that do any work, and of those that devise cunning work.*

a. **Filled** SC OT: a primitive root, to fill or (intransitively) be full of, in a wide application (literally and figuratively)

2. **Solomon's Temple**

a. **Hiram 1 Kings 7:13-14 KJV**

*13 And king Solomon sent and fetched Hiram out of Tyre.*

*14 He was a widow's son of the tribe of Naphtali, and his father was a man of Tyre, a worker in brass: and he was filled with wisdom, and understanding, and cunning to work all works in brass. And he came to king Solomon, and wrought all his work.*

F. **The sixth phrase is "Rested Upon"**

1. **Moses and the seventy elders. Num. 11:25 KJV**

*25 And the LORD came down in a cloud, and spake unto him, and took of the spirit that was upon him, and gave it unto the seventy elders: and it came to pass, that, when the spirit rested upon them, they prophesied, and did not cease.*

2. **Eldad and Medad Num. 11:26 KJV**

*26 But there remained two of the men in the camp, the name of the one was Eldad, and the name of the other Medad: and the spirit rested upon them; and they were of them that were written, but went not out unto the tabernacle: and they prophesied in the camp.*

a. **Rested Upon** SC OT: a primitive root; to rest, i.e. settle down; used in a great variety of applications, literal and figurative, intransitive, transitive and causative (to dwell, stay, let fall, place, let alone, withdraw, give comfort, etc.)

## G. The seventh phrase is "Upon"

### 1. Moses and the seventy elders Num. 11:17 KJV

*17 And I will come down and talk with thee there: and I will take of the spirit which is upon thee, and will put it upon them; and they shall bear the burden of the people with thee, that thou bear it not thyself alone.*

**Num. 11:25** *And the LORD came down in a cloud, and spake unto him, and took of the spirit that was upon him, and gave it unto the seventy elders: and it came to pass, that, when the spirit rested upon them, they prophesied, and did not cease. KJV*

**Num. 11:29** *And Moses said unto him, Enviest thou for my sake? would God that all the LORD's people were prophets, and that the LORD would put his spirit upon them! KJV*

### 2. The Redeemer Isa. 59:20-21 KJV

*20 And the Redeemer shall come to Zion, and unto them that turn from transgression in Jacob, saith the LORD.*
*21 As for me, this is my covenant with them, saith the LORD; My spirit that is upon thee, and my words which I have put in thy mouth, shall not depart out of thy mouth, nor out of the mouth of thy seed, nor out of the mouth of thy seed's seed, saith the LORD, from henceforth and forever.*

### 3. Jesus Christ Isa. 61:1 KJV

*1 The Spirit of the Lord GOD is upon me; because the LORD hath anointed me to preach good tidings unto the meek; he hath sent me to bind up the brokenhearted, to proclaim liberty to the captives, and the opening of the prison to them that are bound;*

a. **Upon** SC OT: above, over, upon, or against (yet always in this last relation with a downward aspect) in a great variety of applications (as follow)

1. SC OT: the top; specifically, the highest (i.e. God); also (adverb) aloft, to Jehovah

2. SC OT: to ascend

## H. The eighth phrase is "In Whom"

### 1. Joshua Num. 27:18 KJV

*18 And the LORD said unto Moses, Take thee Joshua the son of Nun, a man in whom is the spirit, and lay thine hand upon him;*

2. **Daniel Dan. 4:8-9 KJV**

*8 But at the last Daniel came in before me, whose name was Belteshazzar, according to the name of my god, and in whom is the spirit of the holy gods: and before him I told the dream, saying,*
*9 O Belteshazzar, master of the magicians, because I know that the spirit of the holy gods is in thee, and no secret troubleth thee, tell me the visions of my dream that I have seen, and the interpretation thereof.*

3. **Joseph Gen. 41:38 KJV**

*38 An Pharaoh said unto his servants, Can we find such a one as this is, a man in whom the Spirit of God is?*

## I. The ninth phrase is "With"

1. **Caleb Num. 14:24 KJV**

*24 But my servant Caleb, because he had another spirit with him, and hath followed me fully, him will I bring into the land whereinto he went; and his seed shall possess it.*

a. **With** SC OT: a primitive root; to associate; by implication, to overshadow (by huddling together)

## J. The tenth phrase is "Fell upon Men"

1. **Ezekiel Ezek. 11:5 KJV**

*5 And the Spirit of the LORD fell upon me, and said unto me, Speak; Thus saith the LORD; Thus have ye said, O house of Israel: for I know the things that come into your mind, every one of them.*

a. **Fell** SC OT: a primitive root; to fall, in a great variety of applications (intransitive or causative, literal or figurative)

## K. The eleventh phrase is "Within You"

1. **Ezekiel Ezek. 36:27 KJV**

*27 And I will put my spirit within you, and cause you to walk in my statutes, and ye shall keep my judgments, and do them.*

a. **Within** SC OT: properly, the nearest part, i.e. the center, whether literal, figurative or adverbial (especially with preposition)

**b.** SC OT: to approach (causatively, bring near) for whatever purpose

**L. The twelfth phrase is "In You"**

**1. Ezekiel Ezek. 37:14 KJV**

*14 And shall put my spirit in you, and ye shall live, and I shall place you in your own land: then shall ye know that I the LORD have spoken it, and performed it, saith the LORD.*

**2. Joshua Num. 27:18 KJV**

*18 And the LORD said unto Moses, Take thee Joshua the son of Nun, a man in whom is the spirit, and lay thine hand upon him;*

**M. The thirteenth phrase is the Spirit in the prophets Neh. 9:30 KJV**

*30 Yet many years didst thou forbear them, and testifiedst against them by thy spirit in thy prophets: yet would they not give ear: therefore gavest thou them into the hand of the people of the lands.*

**1 Peter 1:10-11 KJV**

*10 Of which salvation the prophets have inquired and searched diligently, who prophesied of the grace that should come unto you:*

*11 Searching what, or what manner of time the Spirit of Christ which was in them did signify, when it testified beforehand the sufferings of Christ, and the glory that should follow.*

**N. The fourteenth phrase is "Remain"**

**1. Haggai Hag. 2:5 KJV**

*5 According to the word that I covenanted with you when ye came out of Egypt, so my spirit remaineth among you: fear ye not.*

**a. Remaineth** SC OT: a primitive root; to stand, in various relations (literal and figurative, intransitive and transitive)

**O. The fifteenth phrase is "moved"**

**1. The Holy Spirit also moved upon each of those who were writing the sacred scriptures of both the Old and the New Testaments. 2 Peter 1:20-21 KJV**

*20 Knowing this first, that no prophecy of the scripture is of any private interpretation.*

*21 For the prophecy came not in old time by the will of man: but holy men of God spake as they were moved by the Holy Ghost.*

1. **Moved** SC NT: to "bear" or carry (in a very wide application, literally and figuratively, as follows)

   **1 Peter 1:10-11 KJV**
   *10 Of which salvation the prophets have inquired and searched diligently, who prophesied of the grace that should come unto you:*
   *11 Searching what, or what manner of time the Spirit of Christ which was in them did signify, when it testified beforehand the sufferings of Christ, and the glory that should follow.*

   **2 Tim. 3:16** *All scripture is given by inspiration of God, and is profitable for doctrine, for reproof, for correction, for instruction in righteousness: KJV*

2. **Inspiration** SC NT: divinely breathed in

# NEW TESTAMENT TITLES & DESCRIPTIONS

I. **There are many titles given to the Holy Spirit which bring truth with each one. These names indicate His character and work. We will look at the titles which are given. There are 18 different titles and descriptions in the New Testament.**

A. **The Holy Spirit Luke 11:13 KJV**

*13 If ye then, being evil, know how to give good gifts unto your children: how much more shall your heavenly Father give the Holy Spirit to them that ask him?*

1. **Holy** SC NT: sacred (physically, pure, morally blameless or religious, ceremonially, consecrated)

2. **Spirit** SC NT: a current of air, i.e. breath (blast) or a breeze; by analogy or figuratively, a spirit, i.e. (human) the rational soul, (by implication) vital principle, mental disposition, etc., or (superhuman) an angel, demon, or (divine) God, Christ's spirit, the Holy Spirit

B. **Spirit of Truth John 14:17 KJV**

*17 Even the Spirit of truth; whom the world cannot receive, because it seeth him not, neither knoweth him: but ye know him; for he dwelleth with you, and shall be in you.*

1. **Truth** SC NT: truth

a. SC NT: true (as not concealing)

**John 17:17** *Sanctify them through thy truth: thy word is truth. KJV*

**John 16:13** *Howbeit when he, the Spirit of truth, is come, he will guide you into all truth: for he shall not speak of himself; but whatsoever he shall hear, that shall he speak: and he will shew you things to come. KJV*

**1 John 4:6** *We are of God: he that knoweth God heareth us; he that is not of God heareth not us. Hereby know we the spirit of truth, and the spirit of error. KJV*

**John 15:26** *But when the Comforter is come, whom I will send unto you from the Father, even the Spirit of truth, which proceedeth from the Father, he shall testify of me: KJV*

1. **Testify** SC NT: to be witness, i.e. testify (literally or figuratively)

    a. SC NT: of uncertain affinity; a witness (literally [judicially] or figuratively [genitive case]); by analogy, a "martyr"

**John 16:13** *Howbeit when he, the Spirit of truth, is come, he will guide you into all truth: for he shall not speak of himself; but whatsoever he shall hear, that shall he speak: and he will shew you things to come. KJV*

1. **Guide** SC NT: to show the way (literally or figuratively [teach])

    a. SC NT: a conductor (literally or figuratively [teacher])

2. **The Spirit of Truth reveals, leads, testifies to, and upholds the truth - The Spirit of Truth opposes the spirit of error 1 John 4:6 KJV**

    *6 We are of God: he that knoweth God heareth us; he that is not of God heareth not us. Hereby know we the spirit of truth, and the spirit of error.*

    a. **Error** SC NT: fraudulence; subjectively, a straying from orthodoxy or piety

    b. SC NT: roving (as a tramp), i.e. (by implication) an impostor or misleader

C. **The Comforter John 15:26 KJV**

*26 But when the Comforter is come, whom I will send unto you from the Father, even the Spirit of truth, which proceedeth from the Father, he shall testify of me:*

1. **Comforter** SC NT: an intercessor, consoler

**John 14:16** *And I will pray the Father, and he shall give you another Comforter, that he may abide with you forever; KJV*

1. **Another** SC NT: allos (al'-los); a primary word; "else," i.e. different (in many applications)

    a. **Vine's Expository Dictionary of Biblical Words**

        1. **Parakletos** lit., "called to one's side," i.e., to one's aid, is primarily a verbal adjective, and suggests the capability or adaptability for giving aid

        2. It was used in a court of justice to denote a legal assistant, counsel for the defense, an advocate; then, generally, one who pleads another's cause, an intercessor, advocate, as in 1 John 2:1, of the Lord Jesus.

3. "**another** (allos, "another of the same sort," not heteros, "different")

**John 14:26** *But the Comforter, which is the Holy Ghost, whom the Father will send in my name, he shall teach you all things, and bring all things to your remembrance, whatsoever I have said unto you. KJV*

**John 15:26** *But when the Comforter is come, whom I will send unto you from the Father, even the Spirit of truth, which proceedeth from the Father, he shall testify of me: KJV*

**John 16:7** *Nevertheless I tell you the truth; It is expedient for you that I go away: for if I go not away, the Comforter will not come unto you; but if I depart, I will send him unto you. KJV*

**1 John 2:1** *My little children, these things write I unto you, that ye sin not. And if any man sin, we have an advocate with the Father, Jesus Christ the righteous: KJV*

**D. The Spirit of Life Rom. 8:2 KJV**

*2 For the law of the Spirit of life in Christ Jesus hath made me free from the law of sin and death.*

**Rev. 11:11** *And after three days and an half the Spirit of life from God entered into them, and they stood upon their feet; and great fear fell upon them which saw them. KJV*

1. **Life** SC NT: life (literally or figuratively)

2. SC NT: a primary verb; to live (literally or figuratively)

**E. The Spirit of him that raised Christ from the dead Rom. 8:11 KJV**

*11 But if the Spirit of him that raised up Jesus from the dead dwell in you, he that raised up Christ from the dead shall also quicken your mortal bodies by his Spirit that dwelleth in you.*

**1 Cor. 6:14** *And God hath both raised up the Lord, and will also raise up us by his own power. KJV*

**F. The Spirit of Adoption Rom. 8:15 KJV**

*15 For ye have not received the spirit of bondage again to fear; but ye have received the Spirit of adoption, whereby we cry, Abba, Father.*

1. **Adoption** SC NT: the placing as a son, i.e. adoption (figuratively, Christian sonship in respect to God)

2. **The New Unger's Bible Dictionary ADOPTION**

**Roman:** Adoption was a familiar social phenomenon, and its initial ceremonies and incidents occupied a large and important place in their laws. By adoption an entire stranger in blood became a member of the family in a higher sense than some of the family kin, emancipated sons, or descendants through females. Such a one assumed the family name, engaged in its sacrificial rites, and became, not by sufferance or at will, but to all intents and purposes, a member of the house of his adoption. The tie thus formed could only be broken through the ceremony of emancipation, and formed as complete a barrier to intermarriage as relationship by blood. At Rome, there were two kinds of adoption, both requiring the adopter to be male and childless: arrogatio and adoption proper. The former could only take place where the person to be adopted was independent (sui juris) and his adopter had no prospect of male offspring. The adopted one became, in the eyes of the law, a new creature. He was born again into a new family. This custom was doubtless referred to by Paul (Rom. 8:14-16).

The ceremony of adoption took place in the presence of seven witnesses. The fictitious sale and resale, and the final "vindication" or claim, were accompanied by the legal formula, and might mean the sale of a son into slavery or his adoption into a new family, according to the words used. The touch of the festuca or ceremonial wand might be accompanied by the formula, "I claim this man as my son," or "I claim this man as my slave." It was the function of the witnesses, upon occasion, to testify that the transaction was in truth the adoption of the child.

Adoption and regeneration are two phases of the same fact, regeneration meaning the reproduction of the filial character, and adoption the restoration of the filial privilege. See Justification; Regeneration.

Adoption is a word of position rather than relationship. The believer's relation to God as a child results from the new birth (John 1:12-13), whereas adoption is the divine act whereby one who is already a child is, through redemption from the law, placed in the position of an adult son (Gal. 4:1-5).

## G. The Spirit of Faith 2 Cor. 4:13 KJV

*13 We having the same spirit of faith, according as it is written, I believed, and therefore have I spoken; we also believe, and therefore speak;*

1. **Faith** SC NT: persuasion, i.e. credence; moral conviction (of religious truth, or the truthfulness of God or a religious teacher), especially reliance upon Christ for salvation; abstractly, constancy in such profession; by extension, the system of religious (Gospel) truth itself

   a. SC NT: a primary verb; to convince (by argument, true or false); by analogy, to pacify or conciliate (by other fair means); reflexively or passively, to assent (to evidence or authority), to rely (by inward certainty)

## H. The Spirit of Promise Eph. 1:13 KJV

*13 In whom ye also trusted, after that ye heard the word of truth, the gospel of your salvation: in whom also after that ye believed, ye were sealed with that Holy Spirit of promise,*

1. **Promise** SC NT: an announcement (for information, assent, or pledge; especially a divine assurance of good)

2. SC NT: to announce upon (reflexively), i.e. (by implication) to engage to do something, to assert something respecting oneself

3. SC NT: (to bring tidings); a messenger; especially an "angel"; by implication, a pastor

**Luke 24:49** *And, behold, I send the promise of my Father upon you: but tarry ye in the city of Jerusalem, until ye be endued with power from on high. KJV*

**Acts 1:4** *And, being assembled together with them, commanded them that they should not depart from Jerusalem, but wait for the promise of the Father, which, saith he, ye have heard of me. KJV*

**Acts 2:33** *Therefore being by the right hand of God exalted, and having received of the Father the promise of the Holy Ghost, he hath shed forth this, which ye now see and hear. KJV*

**Acts 2:39** *For the promise is unto you, and to your children, and to all that are afar off, even as many as the Lord our God shall call. KJV*

**Gal. 3:14** *That the blessing of Abraham might come on the Gentiles through Jesus Christ; that we might receive the promise of the Spirit through faith. KJV*

**Eph. 1:13** *In whom ye also trusted, after that ye heard the word of truth, the gospel of your salvation: in whom also after that ye believed, ye were sealed with that holy Spirit of promise, KJV*

1. **Sealed** SC NT: to stamp (with a signet or private mark) for security or preservation (literally or figuratively); by implication, to keep secret, to attest

    a. SC NT: a signet (as fencing in or protecting from misappropriation); by implication, the stamp impressed (as a mark of privacy, or genuineness), literally or figuratively

    b. SC NT: fence or enclose, i.e. (specifically) to block up (figuratively, to silence)

2. **Nelson's Bible Dictionary JEWELRY**

    a. Most men wore signet rings for business purposes

    b. These rings were engraved with the owner's name or symbol to show authority or ownership Gen. 38:18; Ex. 28:11; Esth. 8:8; Dan. 6:17

    c. The signet rings were worn on the finger or strung around the neck. They were usually made of gold and set with an engraved gem

    d. Signet rings were given as gifts for the tabernacle Ex. 35:22

3. **Nelson's Bible Dictionary SIGNET**

   a. A seal or ring used by an official much like a personal signature to give authority to a document. The Old Testament indicates several uses of the ring seal.

   b. Pharaoh gave his ring to Joseph Gen. 41:42 as a badge of his delegated authority

   c. Ahasuerus gave his ring to the wicked Haman Esth. 3:10, 12, then gave it to Mordecai after Haman's treachery was exposed Esth. 8:2

   d. King Darius of Persia sealed the lion's den after Daniel was placed in it Dan. 6:17

   e. The signet was an emblem of royal authority Gen. 41:42

   f. Zerubbabel, who had been chosen by God to lead the returned captives in Jerusalem Hag. 2:23, as compared to a signet ring, signifying that God had invested him with the highest honor

4. **Nelson's Bible Dictionary SEAL**

   a. A device such as a signet ring or cylinder, engraved with the owner's name, a design, or both Ex. 28:11; Esth. 8:8

   b. A medallion or ring used as a seal featured a raised or recessed signature or symbol so it could be impressed on wax or moist clay to leave its mark Job 38:14

   c. The seal was strung on a cord and hung around the neck or worn on one's finger Gen. 38:18, (RSV; Jer. 22:24)

   d. A seal usually served to certify a signature or authenticate a letter or other document Neh. 9:38; Esth. 8:8; John 3:33

   e. In the New Testament, Pilate authorized a guard to be sent to secure the tomb where the body of Jesus had been laid: "So they went and made the tomb secure, sealing the stone and setting the guard" Matt. 27:66

   f. The word seal is used also in a figurative sense of an outward condition
   John 6:27; 1 Cor. 9:2; 2 Tim. 2:19

   g. The Book of Revelation uses the word frequently in this sense
   Rev. 5:1; 7:2-8; 10:4

**I. The Spirit of Wisdom and Revelation Eph. 1:17 KJV**

*17 That the God of our Lord Jesus Christ, the Father of glory, may give unto you the spirit of wisdom and revelation in the knowledge of him:*

1. **Wisdom** SC NT: wisdom (higher or lower, worldly or spiritual)

2. **Revelation** SC NT: disclosure

    a. SC NT: to take off the cover, i.e. disclose

**J. The Spirit of Glory 1 Pet. 4:14 KJV**

*14 If ye be reproached for the name of Christ, happy are ye; for the spirit of glory and of God resteth upon you: on their part he is evil spoken of, but on your part he is glorified.*

1. **Glory** SC NT: glory (as very apparent), in a wide application (literal or figurative, objective or subjective)

**K. The Spirit of Prophecy Rev.19:10 KJV**

*10 And I fell at his feet to worship him. And he said unto me, See thou do it not: I am thy fellowservant, and of thy brethren that have the testimony of Jesus: worship God: for the testimony of Jesus is the spirit of prophecy.*

1. **Prophecy** SC NT: prediction (scriptural or other)

2. SC NT: a foreteller ("prophet"); by analogy, an inspired speaker; by extension, a poet

3. SC NT: "fore", i.e. in front of, prior (figuratively, superior) to

4. SC NT: to show or make known one's thoughts, i.e. speak or say

**L. The Power of the Highest Luke 1:35 KJV**

*35 And the angel answered and said unto her, The Holy Ghost shall come upon thee, and the power of the Highest shall overshadow thee: therefore also that holy thing which shall be born of thee shall be called the Son of God.*

1. **Power** SC NT: force (literally or figuratively); specially, miraculous power (usually by implication, a miracle itself)

    a. SC NT: to be able or possible

2. **Highest** SC NT: highest, i.e. (masculine singular) the Supreme (God), or (neuter plural) the heavens

3. **Overshadow** SC NT: to cast a shade upon, i.e. (by analogy) to envelope in a haze of brilliancy; figuratively, to invest with preternatural influence

## M. The Spirit of Holiness Rom. 1:4 KJV

*4 And declared to be the Son of God with power, according to the spirit of holiness, by the resurrection from the dead:*

1. **Holiness** SC NT: sacredness (i.e. properly, the quality)

    a. SC NT: (an awful thing); sacred (physically, pure, morally blameless or religious, ceremonially, consecrated)

## N. The Spirit of Love 2 Tim 1:7 KJV (Note: I have included the Greek words for the different expressions of love in the New Testament)

*7 For God hath not given us the spirit of fear; but of power, and of love, and of a sound mind.*

1. **Love** SC NT: agapao (ag-ap-ah'-o); to love (in a social or moral sense)

**John 15:19** *If ye were of the world, the world would love his own: but because ye are not of the world, but I have chosen you out of the world, therefore the world hateth you. KJV*

1. **Love** SC NT: phileo (fil-eh'-o); to be a friend to (fond of [an individual or an object]), i.e. have affection for (denoting personal attachment, as a matter of sentiment or feeling;

    a. SC NT: properly, dear, i.e. a friend; actively, fond, i.e. friendly (still as a noun, an associate, neighbor, etc.)

**Rom. 12:10** *Be kindly affectioned one to another with brotherly love; in honour preferring one another; KJV*

a. **Love** SC NT: 5360 philadelphia (fil-ad-el-fee'-ah); fraternal affection

    1. SC NT: 5361 philadelphos (fil-ad'-el-fos); fond of brethren, i.e. fraternal

    2. SC NT: 5384 philos (fee'-los); properly, dear, i.e. a friend; actively, fond, i.e. friendly (still as a noun, an associate, neighbor, etc.)

**1 Tim. 6:10** *For the love of money is the root of all evil: which while some coveted after, they have erred from the faith, and pierced themselves through with many sorrows. KJV*

a. **Love** SC NT: 5365 philarguria (fil-ar-goo-ree'-ah); avarice

    1. SC NT: 5366 philarguros (fil-ar'-goo-ros); fond of silver (money), i.e. avaricious

**Titus 2:4** *That they may teach the young women to be sober, to love their husbands, to love their children, KJV*

a. **Love** SC NT: 5388 philoteknos (fil-ot'-ek-nos); fond of one's children, i.e. maternal

## O. An Unction from the Holy One 1 John 2:20 KJV

*20 But ye have an unction from the Holy One, and ye know all things.*

1. **Unction** SC NT: an unguent or smearing, i.e. (figuratively) the special endowment ("chrism") of the Holy Spirit

   a. SC NT: through the idea of contact; to smear or rub with oil, i.e. (by implication) to consecrate to an office or religious service

   b. SC NT: a primary verb (perhaps rather from NT: 5495, to handle); to furnish what is needed; (give an oracle, "graze" [touch slightly], light upon, etc.), i.e. (by implication) to employ or (by extension) to act towards one in a given manner

## P. The Anointing 1 John 2:27 KJV

*27 But the anointing which ye have received of him abideth in you, and ye need not that any man teach you: but as the same anointing teacheth you of all things, and is truth, and is no lie, and even as it hath taught you, ye shall abide in him.*

1. **Anointing** SC NT: an unguent or smearing, i.e. (figuratively) the special endowment ("chrism") of the Holy Spirit

2. SC NT: through the idea of contact; to smear or rub with oil, i.e. (by implication) to consecrate to an office or religious service

3. SC NT: a primary verb (perhaps rather from NT: 5495, to handle); to furnish what is needed; (give an oracle, "graze" [touch slightly], light upon, etc.), i.e. (by implication) to employ or (by extension) to act towards one in a given manner

## Q. The Spirit Matt. 4:1 KJV

*1 Then was Jesus led up of the Spirit into the wilderness to be tempted of the devil.*

**Mark 1:10** *And straightway coming up out of the water, he saw the heavens opened, and the Spirit like a dove descending upon him: KJV*

**Luke 2:27** *And he came by the Spirit into the temple: and when the parents brought in the child Jesus, to do for him after the custom of the law, KJV*

**R. Spirit of God Rom. 15:19 KJV**

*19 Through mighty signs and wonders, by the power of the Spirit of God; so that from Jerusalem, and round about unto Illyricum, I have fully preached the gospel of Christ.*

**S. The Spirit of our God I Cor. 6:11 KJV**

*11 And such were some of you: but ye are washed, but ye are sanctified, but ye are justified in the name of the Lord Jesus, and by the Spirit of our God.*

**T. The Spirit of the living God 2 Cor. 3:3 KJV**

*3 Forasmuch as ye are manifestly declared to be the epistle of Christ ministered by us, written not with ink, but with the Spirit of the living God; not in tables of stone, but in fleshy tables of the heart.*

**U. The Spirit of Jesus Christ Phil. 1:19 KJV**

*19 For I know that this shall turn to my salvation through your prayer, and the supply of the Spirit of Jesus Christ,*

**V. The Spirit of Christ 1 Pet. 1:11 KJV**

*11 Searching what, or what manner of time the Spirit of Christ which was in them did signify, when it testified beforehand the sufferings of Christ, and the glory that should follow.*

**Rom. 8:9** *But ye are not in the flesh, but in the Spirit, if so be that the Spirit of God dwell in you. Now if any man have not the Spirit of Christ, he is none of his. KJV*

**W. The Holy Spirit of God Eph. 4:30 KJV**

*30 And grieve not the Holy Spirit of God, whereby ye are sealed unto the day of redemption.*

**X. The Spirit of his Son Gal. 4:6 KJV**

*6 And because ye are sons, God hath sent forth the Spirit of his Son into your hearts, crying, Abba, Father.*

**Y. The Spirit which is of God 1 Cor. 2:12 KJV**

*12 Now we have received, not the spirit of the world, but the spirit which is of God; that we might know the things that are freely given to us of God.*

**Z. The Consolation of Israel Luke 2:25 AMP**

*25 Now there was a man in Jerusalem whose name was Simeon, and this man was righteous and devout [cautiously and carefully observing the divine Law], and looking for the Consolation of Israel; and the Holy Spirit was upon him.*

1. **Consolation** SC NT: imploration, hortation, solace

    a. **SC NT:** to call near, i.e. invite, invoke (by imploration, hortation or consolation)

2. **Barnes' Notes**

    [Waiting for the consolation of Israel] That is, waiting for the "Messiah," who is called "the consolation of Israel" because he would give comfort to them by his appearing. This term was often applied to the Messiah before he actually appeared. It was common to swear, also, by "the consolation of Israel" - that is, by the Messiah about to come. See Lightfoot on this place.

3. **Adam Clarke's Commentary Luke 2:25**

    [Waiting for the consolation of Israel] That is, the Messiah, who was known among the pious Jews by this character: he was to be the consolation of Israel, because he was to be its redemption. This consolation of Israel was so universally expected that the Jews swore by it: So let me see the Consolation, if such a thing be not so, or so. See the forms in Lightfoot.

4. **Jamieson, Fausset, and Brown Commentary Luke 2:25**

    And the same man was just (upright in his moral character), and devout (of a religious frame of spirit), waiting for the consolation of Israel - or, for the Messiah; a beautiful and pregnant title of the promised Savior:

5. **The Wycliffe Bible Commentary Luke 2:25**

    The Consolation of Israel. The expected Messiah, who would deliver the Jews from their oppressors.

# IN CREATION

## INTRO:

**The Holy Spirit is seen as early as the second verse of Genesis 1:1-2 KJV**

*1 In the beginning God created the heaven and the earth.*
*2 And the earth was without form, and void; and darkness was upon the face of the deep. And the Spirit of God moved upon the face of the waters.*

**The Holy Spirit was involved with all of creation. The person of "God" created everything in Genesis. Thirty-two times the godhead is mentioned in the creation story. Everything that was created was brought into being by all three, Father, Son, and the Holy Spirit.**

1. **In the book of Genesis the word God is used in the creation account**

    a. Genesis chapter one: 32 times

    b. Genesis chapter two 14 times

    c. Genesis chapter three 12 times Total 58 times

2. **The first insight into the meaning of the word God is found in Gen. 1:26 KJV**

    *26 And God said, Let us make man in our image, after our likeness: and let them have dominion over the fish of the sea, and over the fowl of the air, and over the cattle, and over all the earth, and over every creeping thing that creepeth upon the earth. KJV*

    a. The word God is connected with "let US" make man – signaling more than one

3. **Strongs Concordance defines God as elohiym – plural – more than one**

    a. **God** SC OT: plural of OT: 433; gods in the ordinary sense; but specifically used (in the plural thus, especially with the article) of the supreme God

4. **Barnes' Notes Gen 1:2**

This character seldom consists of one quality; usually, if not universally, of more than one. Hence, in the Eternal One may and must be that CHARACTER which is the concentration of all the causative antecedents of a universe of things. The first of these is WILL. Without free choice there can be no beginning of things. Hence, matter cannot be a creator. But will needs, cannot be without, WISDOM to plan and POWER to execute what is to be WILLED. These are the three essential attributes of SPIRIT. The manifold wisdom of the Eternal Spirit, combined with His equally manifold power, is adequate to the creation of a manifold system of things. Let the free behest be given, and the universe starts into being.

Nothing but a creative or absolutely initiative power could give rise to a change so great and fundamental as the construction of an Adamic abode out of the luminous, aerial, aqueous, and terrene materials of the preexistent earth, and the production of the new vegetable and animal species with which it was now to be replenished.

5. **The Spirit of God moved, brood, flutter, shake or move upon the face of the waters**

   a. **Moved** SC OT: a primitive root; to brood; by implication, to be relaxed

      1. This word is also used as flutter, move, or shake

   b. **It was the power and creativity of the Spirit that brought the earthly contents within the water to come forth and make the dry land or solid earth 2 Peter 3:5 AMP**

      *5 For they willfully overlook and forget this [fact], that the heavens [came into] existence long ago by the word of God, and the earth also which was formed out of water and by means of water,*

I. **In Genesis 1:1 to Genesis 2:2 God created all of the following:**

*1 In the beginning God created the **Heaven** and the **earth.***
*2 And the earth was without form, and void; and darkness was upon the face of the deep. And the Spirit of God moved upon the face of the **waters**.*
*3 And God said, Let there be **light:** and there was light.*
*4 And God saw the light, that it was good: and God divided the light from the **darkness**.*
*5 And God called the **light Day**, and the **darkness he called Night**. And **the evening and the morning were the first day.***
*6 And God said, Let there be a **firmament** in the midst of the **waters,** and let it divide the waters from the waters.*
*7 And God made the firmament, and divided the waters which were under the firmament from the waters which were above the firmament: and it was so.*
*8 And God called the firmament **Heaven**. And **the evening and the morning were the second day**.*
*9 And God said, Let the waters under the heaven be gathered together unto one place, and let the dry land appear: and it was so.*
*10 And God called the dry land **Earth**; and the gathering together of the waters called he **Seas**: and God saw that it was good.*

*11 And God said, Let the earth bring forth* ***grass****, the* ***herb yielding seed****, and the* ***fruit tree*** *yielding fruit after his kind, whose seed is in itself, upon the earth: and it was so.*

*12 And the earth brought forth grass, and herb yielding seed after his kind, and the tree yielding fruit, whose seed was in itself, after his kind: and God saw that it was good.*

*13 And* ***the evening and the morning were the third day****.*

*14 And God said, Let there be* ***lights in the firmament of the heaven*** *to divide the day from the night; and let them be for signs, and for seasons, and for days, and years:*

*15 And let them be for lights in the firmament of the heaven to give light upon the earth: and it was so.*

*16 And God made* ***two great lights****; the greater light to rule the day, and the lesser light to rule the night: he made the* ***stars*** *also.*

*17 And God set them in the firmament of the heaven to give light upon the earth,*

*18 And to rule over the day and over the night, and to divide the light from the darkness: and God saw that it was good.*

*19 And* ***the evening and the morning were the fourth day****.*

*20 And God said, Let the waters bring forth abundantly* ***the moving creature*** *that hath life, and* ***fowl*** *that may fly above the earth in the open firmament of heaven.*

*21 And God created* ***great whales****, and* ***every living creature that moveth****, which the waters brought forth abundantly, after their kind, and every winged fowl after his kind: and God saw that it was good.*

*22 And God blessed them, saying, Be fruitful, and multiply, and fill the waters in the seas, and let fowl multiply in the earth.*

*23 And* ***the evening and the morning were the fifth day****.*

*24 And God said, Let the earth bring forth* ***the living creature after his kind****,* ***cattle****, and* ***creeping thing****, and* ***beast of the earth*** *after his kind: and it was so.*

*25 And God made the* ***beast*** *of the earth after his kind, and* ***cattle*** *after their kind, and* ***everything that creepeth*** *upon the earth after his kind: and God saw that it was good.*

*26 And God said, Let us* ***make man in our image, after our likeness****: and let them have dominion over the fish of the sea, and over the fowl of the air, and over the cattle, and over all the earth, and over every creeping thing that creepeth upon the earth.*

*27 So God created man in his own image, in the image of God created he him;* ***male and female*** *created he them.*

*28 And God blessed them, and God said unto them, Be fruitful, and multiply, and replenish the earth, and subdue it: and have dominion over the fish of the sea, and over the fowl of the air, and over every living thing that moveth upon the earth.*

*29 And God said, Behold, I have given you every herb bearing seed, which is upon the face of all the earth, and every tree, in the which is the fruit of a tree yielding seed; to you it shall be for meat.*

*30 And to every beast of the earth, and to every fowl of the air, and to everything that creepeth upon the earth, wherein there is life, I have given every green herb for meat: and it was so.*

*31 And God saw everything that he had made, and, behold, it was very good. And* ***the evening and the morning were the sixth day****.*

**Gen. 2:1-2 KJV**

*1 Thus the* ***heavens*** *and the earth were finished,* ***and all the host of them****.*

*2 And on* ***the seventh day*** *God ended his work which he had made; and he rested on the seventh day from all his work which he had made.*

## II. Throughout scripture there are references to God in creation

### A. Light and Darkness Isa. 45:7 KJV

*7 I form the light, and create darkness: I make peace, and create evil: I the LORD do all these things.*

### B. The creation of the Earth – note verse 13 the Spirit of the LORD Isa. 40:12-14 KJV

*12 Who hath measured the waters in the hollow of his hand, and meted out heaven with the span, and comprehended the dust of the earth in a measure, and weighed the mountains in scales, and the hills in a balance?*
*13 Who hath directed the Spirit of the LORD, or being his counseller hath taught him?*
*14 With whom took he counsel, and who instructed him, and taught him in the path of judgment, and taught him knowledge, and shewed to him the way of understanding?*

### C. By the word of the Lord and by the breath of his mouth Ps. 33:6-9 KJV

*6 By the word of the LORD were the heavens made; and all the host of them by the breath of his mouth.*
*7 He gathereth the waters of the sea together as an heap: he layeth up the depth in storehouses.*
*8 Let all the earth fear the LORD: let all the inhabitants of the world stand in awe of him.*
*9 For he spake, and it was done; he commanded, and it stood fast.*

#### 1. The breath of God relates to the Spirit John 20:22 KJV

*22 And when he had said this, he breathed on them, and saith unto them, Receive ye the Holy Ghost:*

### D. Man Job 33:4 KJV

*4 The Spirit of God hath made me, and the breath of the Almighty hath given me life.*

### E. The animals Ps. 104:24-30 AMP

*24 O Lord, how many and varied are Your works! In wisdom have You made them all; the earth is full of Your riches and Your creatures.*
*25 Yonder is the sea, great and wide, in which are swarms of innumerable creeping things, creatures both small and great.*
*26 There go the ships of the sea, and Leviathan (the sea monster), which You have formed to sport in it.*
*27 These all wait and are dependent upon You, that You may give them their food in due season.*
*28 When You give it to them, they gather it up; You open Your hand, and they are filled with good things.*
*29 When You hide Your face, they are troubled and dismayed; when You take away their breath, they die and return to their dust.*
*30 When You send forth Your Spirit and give them breath, they are created, and You replenish the face of the ground.*

# Conclusion: Job 26:7-14 AMP

*7 He it is Who spreads out the northern skies over emptiness and hangs the earth upon or over nothing.*

*8 He holds the waters bound in His clouds [which otherwise would spill on earth all at once], and the cloud is not rent under them.*

*9 He covers the face of His throne and spreads over it His cloud.*

*10 He has placed an enclosing limit [the horizon] upon the waters at the boundary between light and darkness.*

*11 The pillars of the heavens tremble and are astonished at His rebuke.*

*12 He stills or stirs up the sea by His power, and by His understanding He smites proud Rahab.*

*13 By His breath the heavens are garnished; His hand pierced the [swiftly] fleeing serpent. [Ps. 33:6.]*

*14 Yet these are but [a small part of His doings] the outskirts of His ways or the mere fringes of His force, the faintest whisper of His voice! Who dares contemplate or who can understand the thunders of His full, magnificent power?*

# SYMBOL - DOVE

## INTRO:

**In scripture, there are nine different symbols that represent the Holy Spirit. All of these symbols present a different side of truth concerning the third person of the trinity.**

A symbol is something that represents something else by association, resemblance, or convention, especially a material object used to represent something invisible.

In this study, we will consider nine different symbols of the Holy Spirit

Each symbol that is used must have scripture that ties the two together (Symbol and the Holy Spirit)

| | | |
|---|---|---|
| Dove | Matt. 3:16 | 1st Symbol |
| River | John 7:38-39 | 2nd Symbol |
| Water | Isa. 44:1-3 | 3rd Symbol |
| Rain | Joel 2:23-29 | 4th Symbol |
| Fire | Matt. 3:11, Acts 2:3-4 | 5th Symbol |
| Wind | Acts 2:1-4 | 6th Symbol |
| Seal | 2 Cor. 1:21, Eph. 1:13-14 | 7th Symbol |
| Oil | 1 Sam. 16:13 | 8th Symbol |
| Breath | John 20:22 | 9th Symbol |

**I. The first symbol that will be considered is the Dove**

**A. When Jesus came to John the Baptist for water baptism the Spirit came upon Him in the form of a dove. Matt. 3:16 KJV**

*16 And Jesus, when he was baptized, went up straightway out of the water: and, lo, the heavens were opened unto him, and he saw the Spirit of God descending like a dove, and lighting upon him:*

**Mark 1:10** *And straightway coming up out of the water, he saw the heavens opened, and the Spirit like a dove descending upon him: KJV*

**Luke 3:22** *And the Holy Ghost descended in a bodily shape like a dove upon him, and a voice came from heaven, which said, Thou art my beloved Son; in thee I am well pleased. KJV*

**John 1:33** *And I knew him not: but he that sent me to baptize with water, the same said unto me, Upon whom thou shalt see the Spirit descending, and remaining on him, the same is he which baptizeth with the Holy Ghost. KJV*

**II. The nature of the dove is as follows:**

**A. The dove is not a bird of prey consequently it has a gentle spirit**

**Gal. 5:22** *But the fruit of the Spirit is love, joy, peace, longsuffering, gentleness, goodness, faith, KJV*

**2 Sam. 22:36** *Thou hast also given me the shield of thy salvation: and thy gentleness hath made me great. KJV*

**Ps. 18:35** *Thou hast also given me the shield of thy salvation: and thy right hand hath holden me up, and thy gentleness hath made me great. KJV*

**2 Cor. 10:1** *Now I Paul myself beseech you by the meekness and gentleness of Christ, who in presence am base among you, but being absent am bold toward you: KJV*

**B. The dove is harmless Matt. 10:16 KJV**

*16 Behold, I send you forth as sheep in the midst of wolves: be ye therefore wise as serpents, and harmless as doves.*

1. **Harmless** SC NT: unmixed, i.e. (figuratively) innocent

**C. The dove is a symbol of purity. They were used for sacrifices for purification Luke 2:23-24 KJV**

*23(As it is written in the law of the Lord, Every male that openeth the womb shall be called holy to the Lord)*
*24 And to offer a sacrifice according to that which is said in the law of the Lord, A pair of turtledoves, or two young pigeons.*

**Gen. 15:9** *And he said unto him, Take me an heifer of three years old, and a she goat of three years old, and a ram of three years old, and a turtledove, and a young pigeon. KJV*

**Lev. 1:14** *And if the burnt sacrifice for his offering to the LORD be of fowls, then he shall bring his offering of turtledoves, or of young pigeons. KJV*

**Lev. 5:7** *And if he be not able to bring a lamb, then he shall bring for his trespass, which he hath committed, two turtledoves, or two young pigeons, unto the LORD; one for a sin offering, and the other for a burnt offering. KJV*

**Lev. 5:11** *But if he be not able to bring two turtledoves, or two young pigeons, then he that sinned shall bring for his offering the tenth part of an ephah of fine flour for a sin offering; he shall put no oil upon it, neither shall he put any frankincense thereon: for it is a sin offering. KJV*

**Lev. 14:22** *And two turtledoves, or two young pigeons, such as he is able to get; and the one shall be a sin offering, and the other a burnt offering. KJV*

**Lev. 14:30** *And he shall offer the one of the turtledoves, or of the young pigeons, such as he can get; KJV*

D. **The voice of the dove is a soft cooing sound. It is a sound of peace. Neh. 2:14 KJV**

*14 O my dove, that art in the clefts of the rock, in the secret places of the stairs, let me see thy countenance, let me hear thy voice; for sweet is thy voice, and thy countenance is comely.*

**Isa. 38:14** *Like a crane or a swallow, so did I chatter: I did mourn as a dove: mine eyes fail with looking upward: O LORD, I am oppressed; undertake for me. KJV*

1. **Mourn** SC OT: to murmur (in pleasure or anger); by implication, to ponder

**Isa. 59:11** *We roar all like bears, and mourn sore like doves: we look for judgment, but there is none; for salvation, but it is far off from us. KJV*

**Ezek 7:16** *But they that escape of them shall escape, and shall be on the mountains like doves of the valleys, all of them mourning, every one for his iniquity. KJV*

E. **The dove can only see, or focus on one thing at a time. Their vision is limited to just one thing. The Spirit shows us just one thing, CHRIST.**

**John 15:26** *But when the Comforter is come, whom I will send unto you from the Father, even the Spirit of truth, which proceedeth from the Father, he shall testify of me: KJV*

**John 16:13-14 KJV**
*13 Howbeit when he, the Spirit of truth, is come, he will guide you into all truth: for he shall not speak of himself; but whatsoever he shall hear, that shall he speak: and he will shew you things to come.*
*14 He shall glorify me: for he shall receive of mine, and shall shew it unto you.*

**Phil. 3:13-15 KJV**

*13 Brethren, I count not myself to have apprehended: but this one thing I do, forgetting those things which are behind, and reaching forth unto those things which are before,*
*14 I press toward the mark for the prize of the high calling of God in Christ Jesus.*
*15 Let us therefore, as many as be perfect, be thus minded: and if in anything ye be otherwise minded, God shall reveal even this unto you.*

**Luke 10:39-42 KJV**
*39 And she had a sister called Mary, which also sat at Jesus' feet, and heard his word.*
*40 But Martha was cumbered about much serving, and came to him, and said, Lord, dost thou not care that my sister hath left me to serve alone? bid her therefore that she help me.*
*41 And Jesus answered and said unto her, Martha, Martha, thou art careful and troubled about many things:*
*42 But one thing is needful: and Mary hath chosen that good part, which shall not be taken away from her.*

**Ps. 27:4** *One thing have I desired of the LORD, that will I seek after; that I may dwell in the house of the LORD all the days of my life, to behold the beauty of the LORD, and to inquire in his temple. KJV*

**F. The dove must have a resting place. Noah sent out a dove to determine if the waters had receded from the earth. Only when she found a place to rest did she not return. Gen. 8:8-12 KJV**

*8 Also he sent forth a dove from him, to see if the waters were abated from off the face of the ground;*
*9 But the dove found no rest for the sole of her foot, and she returned unto him into the ark, for the waters were on the face of the whole earth: then he put forth his hand, and took her, and pulled her in unto him into the ark.*
*10 And he stayed yet other seven days; and again he sent forth the dove out of the ark;*
*11 And the dove came into him in the evening; and, lo, in her mouth was an olive leaf pluckt off: so Noah knew that the waters were abated from off the earth.*
*12 And he stayed yet other seven days; and sent forth the dove; which returned not again unto him anymore.*

**G. Holman Bible Dictionary**

1. The dove of Palestine was a migratory bird. They could fly long distances and with great speed. They spend the months of April to October in the Holy Land, filling the air with a soft cooing when they arrive each spring (Song 2:11-12).

   **Ps. 55:6-8 KJV**
   *6 And I said, Oh that I had wings like a dove! for then would I fly away, and be at rest.*
   *7 Lo, then would I wander far off, and remain in the wilderness. Selah.*
   *8 I would hasten my escape from the windy storm and tempest.*

**H. The dove makes its nest in the rocks. Jer. 48:28 KJV**

*28 O ye that dwell in Moab, leave the cities, and dwell in the rock, and be like the dove that maketh her nest in the sides of the hole's mouth.*

## III. Holman Bible Dictionary

### A. Because of the gentleness and faithfulness of the dove to its mate, this bird is used as a descriptive title of one's beloved in the Song of Solomon (2:14; 5:2; 6:9).

**Song 2:14** *O my dove, that art in the clefts of the rock, in the secret places of the stairs, let me see thy countenance, let me hear thy voice; for sweet is thy voice, and thy countenance is comely. KJV*

**Song 5:2** *I sleep, but my heart waketh: it is the voice of my beloved that knocketh, saying, Open to me, my sister, my love, my dove, my undefiled: for my head is filled with dew, and my locks with the drops of the night. KJV*

**Song 6:9** *My dove, my undefiled is but one; she is the only one of her mother, she is the choice one of her that bare her. The daughters saw her, and blessed her; yea, the queens and the concubines, and they praised her. KJV*

### B. When the turtledove arrived it signified the arrival of spring. When the Holy Spirit comes into our life a new season begins! Song 2:12; Jer. 8:7.

**Song 2:12** *The flowers appear on the earth; the time of the singing of birds is come, and the voice of the turtle is heard in our land; KJV*

**Jer. 8:7** *Yea, the stork in the heaven knoweth her appointed times; and the turtle and the crane and the swallow observe the time of their coming; but my people know not the judgment of the LORD. KJV*

### C. Dove's Dung

1. Several theories have been formulated to explain the difficulty in regard to this material as an article of food (2 Kings 6:25)

2. That it was a kind of plant, such as one known by that name to the Arabs. But it is unlikely that any plant would have been found in any quantity in a place in the last extremity of famine

3. That it was in reality dung but used as a fertilizer, to promote the quick growth of vegetables for food. This is fanciful and not supported by the context

4. That the people, in the depth of their despair and starvation, actually ate this disgusting material. This seems the most probable view and is supported by the fact that a similar occurrence took place in the English army in 1316

## IV. The New Unger's Bible Dictionary ANIMAL KINGDOM

### A. Dove. (Heb. yona; Grk. peristera)

B. **Four species of wild pigeons are found in Bible lands, the ring dove, or wood pigeon, the stock dove, the rock dove, and the ash-rumped rock dove**

C. **They are all known by the Arab. name of hamam**

D. **They also nest in trees**

E. **They are timid. Hos. 11:11 KJV**

*11 They shall tremble as a bird out of Egypt, and as a dove out of the land of Assyria: and I will place them in their houses, saith the LORD.*

1. **Tremble** SC OT: to shudder with terror; hence, to fear; also to hasten (with anxiety)

F. **The dove is considered to be clean and is used for food**

V. **Nelson's Illustrated Bible Dictionary**

A. **Pigeons were probably the first domesticated bird**

B. **When people realized doves could travel long distances and always find their way home, they used them to carry messages.**

C. **Homing pigeons have keen eyes with which they spot landmarks to help them stay on the right route.**

D. **Doves appear to express affection by stroking each other and "billing and cooing."**

E. **They mate for life, sharing nesting and parenting duties**

F. **They are gentle birds that never resist attack or retaliate against their enemies**

G. **Even when her young are attacked, a dove will give only a pitiful call of distress**

H. **The dove also symbolizes peace, love, forgiveness, and the church**

# RIVER

## INTRO:

**Another symbol for the Holy Spirit is water in the form of a river. The scripture that makes the symbol river with the Holy Spirit is found in John 7:38-39 KJV**

*38 He that believeth on me, as the scripture hath said, out of his belly shall flow rivers of living water.*
*39(But this spake he of the Spirit, which they that believe on him should receive: for the Holy Ghost was not yet given; because that Jesus was not yet glorified.)*

1. **Rivers** SC NT: a current, brook, or freshet (as drinkable), i.e. running water

   a. It is the Greek word potamos from which we get our word potable. Potable means fit to drink or drinkable.

2. SC NT: to imbibe (literally or figuratively)

   a. Imbibe means to drink, also to take in with the senses, drink in

   b. To absorb (moisture)

   c. To take into the mind and keep, as ideas, principles, etc.

3. SC NT: a drinking-bout or carousal

**I. The Old Testament has much about rivers**

**A. There was a river in the garden of Eden Gen. 2:10 KJV**

*10 And a river went out of Eden to water the garden; and from thence it was parted, and became into four heads.*

1. **River** SC OT: a stream (including the sea; especially the Nile, Euphrates, etc.); figuratively, prosperity

   a. SC OT: to sparkle, i.e. (figuratively) be cheerful; hence (from the sheen of a running stream) to flow, i.e. (figuratively) assemble

**B. The purpose of the river was to water the garden**

**1. Water** SC OT: to quaff, i.e. (causatively) to irrigate or furnish a potion to

**a. Brown-Driver-Briggs Hebrew Lexicon**

**1.** To give to drink, to irrigate, to drink, to water, to cause to drink water

**C. The river supplied an overabundance so the garden could drink deeply of the source**

**D. The garden also represents the bride of Christ Song 4:12-16 AMP**

*12 A garden enclosed and barred is my sister, my [promised] bride--a spring shut up, a fountain sealed.*
*13 Your shoots are an orchard of pomegranates or a paradise with precious fruits, henna with spikenard plants, [John 15:5; Eph. 5:9.]*
*14 spikenard and saffron, calamus and cinnamon, with all trees of frankincense, myrrh, and aloes, with all the chief spices.*
*15 You are a fountain [springing up] in a garden, a well of living waters, and flowing streams from Lebanon. [John 4:10; 7:37, 38.]*
*16[You have called me a garden, she said] Oh, I pray that the [cold] north wind and the [soft] south wind may blow upon my garden, that its spices may flow out [in abundance for you in whom my soul delights]. Let my beloved come into his garden and eat its choicest fruits.*

**Jer. 31:12** *They shall come and sing aloud on the height of Zion and shall flow together and be radiant with joy over the goodness of the Lord--for the corn, for the juice [of the grape], for the oil, and for the young of the flock and the herd. And their life shall be like a watered garden, and they shall not sorrow or languish anymore at all. AMP*

**Isa. 58:11** *And the LORD shall guide thee continually, and satisfy thy soul in drought, and make fat thy bones: and thou shalt be like a watered garden, and like a spring of water, whose waters fail not. KJV*

**E. As individuals we can drink of the Spirit of God and find a refreshing, satisfaction and fulfillment in Him Eph. 5:18-19 KJV**

*18 And be not drunk with wine, wherein is excess; but be filled with the Spirit;*
*19 Speaking to yourselves in psalms and hymns and spiritual songs, singing and making melody in your heart to the Lord;*

*18 And do not get drunk with wine, for that is debauchery; but ever be filled and stimulated with the [Holy] Spirit. [Prov. 23:20.]*
*19 Speak out to one another in psalms and hymns and spiritual songs, offering praise with voices [and instruments] and making melody with all your heart to the Lord, AMP*

1. **Filled SC NT:**

| | |
|---|---|
| **a.** To make replete i.e. (literally) to cram (a net) | Luke 5:1-7 |
| **b.** Level up (a hollow) | Luke 3:4-6 |
| **c.** Or (figuratively) to furnish (or imbue, diffuse, influence) | 2 Tim. 3:16-17<br>Acts 19:41 |
| **d.** Satisfy | Ps. 145:16 |
| **e.** Execute (an office) | Acts 13:1-4; 1<br>1 Tim. 3:1-13 |
| **f.** Finish (a period or task) | 2 Tim. 4:7 |
| **g.** Verify (or coincide with a prediction) | Acts 9:10-17 |
| **2. SC NT:** replete, or covered over; by analogy, complete | Eph. 3:19; 4:11-13 |
| **3. SC NT:** to "fill" (literally or figuratively [imbue, influence, supply]) | Phil. 1:19; 2:30 |
| **a.** Specifically, to fulfil (time) | Gal. 4:4; Eph. 1:10 |

**F. The river parted and became four rivers – All lands and people groups need the river to flow to them Gen. 2:11-14 KJV**

*11 The name of the first is Pison: that is it which compasseth the whole land of Havilah, where there is gold;*
*12 And the gold of that land is good: there is bdellium and the onyx stone.*
*13 And the name of the second river is Gihon: the same is it that compasseth the whole land of Ethiopia.*
*14 And the name of the third river is Hiddekel: that is it which goeth toward the east of Assyria. And the fourth river is Euphrates.*

**G. A river flows from its point of origin to the sea – Once again the sea is humanity. The river's purpose is always involved mankind Prov. 8:1-4 KJV**

*1 Doth not wisdom cry? and understanding put forth her voice?*
*2 She standeth in the top of high places, by the way in the places of the paths.*
*3 She crieth at the gates, at the entry of the city, at the coming in at the doors.*
*4 Unto you, O men, I call; and my voice is to the sons of man.*

**II. Rivers were boundary marks for the promise land. Every truth that is revealed is like a river, which sets a new boundary in our lives Gen. 15:18 KJV**

*18 In the same day the LORD made a covenant with Abram, saying, Unto thy seed have I given this land, from the river of Egypt unto the great river, the river Euphrates:*

**Josh. 1:4** *From the wilderness and this Lebanon even unto the great river, the river Euphrates, all the land of the Hittites, and unto the great sea toward the going down of the sun, shall be your coast. KJV*

1. **Euphrates** SC OT: to break forth; rushing; Perath (i.e. Euphrates), a river of the East

**A. In the Biblical time life revolved around the river. It is still the same in this day and age.**

**III. Holman Bible Dictionary RIVER**

RIVERS AND WATERWAYS IN THE BIBLE From the earliest efforts at permanent settlement in the Ancient Near East, people were attracted to the rivers and streams that ultimately would dictate population distribution between the mountains, deserts, and the seas.

The flood plains of many of these rivers originally were inhospitable with thick, tangled jungles, wild beasts, and unpredictable flooding and disease. However, within the areas of plain and lowland that provided a more constant food supply and ease of movement, the need for a permanent water source attracted settlers to the river banks.

Thus the early river civilizations of the Nile, the Tigris, and the Euphrates starting about 3000 B.C., and the Indus civilization slightly later resulted in response to the challenges and benefits these important waterways presented.

Flood control, social and economic organization, and the invention of writing as a means of communication developed.

Trade was facilitated by means of navigable waterways.

Since roads followed the lines of least resistance, the pattern of early trade routes conformed closely, especially in more rugged terrain, to channels and courses of the rivers and streams, and along the shoreline where the earliest fishing villages developed.

Rivers and Streams Each of the biblical rivers was developed to meet distinct human needs. A study of rivers helps understand the culture near the river.

1. **Nile River**

The name Nile is not explicitly mentioned in KJV, but modern translations most often translated the Hebrew yeor as the Nile. The Nile plays a prominent role in the early events in the life of Moses in Exodus (Moses, Ex. 2:3; the ten plagues, Ex. 7:15, 20). The Nile is alluded to in many other passages as "the river" (Gen. 41:1), the "river of Egypt" (Gen. 15:18), the "flood of Egypt" (Amos 8:8), Shihor (Josh. 13:3), river of Cush among other names. The "brook of Egypt" mostly is a reference to Wadi el-Arish, the drainage system of the central Sinai. The prophets Amos (8:8; 9:5) and Jeremiah (46:8) used the Nile as the symbol of Egypt, a concept that is readily understood in terms of the river's historical importance to the survival and well-being of the country.

For the Egyptians, the predictable annual flooding of the Nile with the depositing of the fertile black alluvial soil meant the enrichment of the flood plain and the difference between food and famine. From the central highlands of East Africa, the Nile with a watershed of over one million square miles is formed by the union of the White and Blue Niles and flows a distance of nearly 3,500 miles. From its low ebb at the end of May, the flow of the river gradually rises to its maximum flood stage at the beginning of September. Historically, approximately 95 percent of Egypt's population depended upon the productivity of the 5 percent of the country's land area within the floodplain of the Nile. In the Delta, at least three major branches facilitated irrigation in the extensive fan north of Memphis, the ancient capital of Lower Egypt. See Egypt; Nile.

## 2. The Euphrates

First mentioned in Gen. 2:14 as one of the four branches of the river that watered the Garden of Eden, the Euphrates flows 1,700 miles to become the longest river in Western Asia. From the mountainous region of northeastern Turkey. Armenia), it flows southward into northern Syria and turns southeasterly to join the Tigris and flows into the Persian Gulf. On the Middle Euphrates, Carchemish, originally the center of a small city-state, became the important provincial capital of the Mitanni kingdom, later of the Hittite and Assyrian Empires. At Carchemish in 605 B.C. Nebuchadnezzar II defeated Pharaoh Necho as he began his successful drive to claim the former Assyrian Empire for Babylon (2 Kings 24:7; Jer. 46:1). Two important tributaries, the Belikh and Khabur, flow into the Euphrates from the north before it continues on to the ancient trade center at Marl. The Lower Euphrates generally formed the western limits of the city-states that made up the early Sumerian civilization. From the river plain to the delta, both the Tigris and Euphrates rivers regularly have formed new branches and changed their courses. About 90 percent of their flow mysteriously is lost to irrigation, evaporation, pools and lakes, and the swamps and never reaches the Persian Gulf. Lost as well in this region are the vast amounts of sediment that the Tigris and Euphrates bring from the mountainous regions. Sediment deposits along the lower courses of these rivers average 16 to 23 feet with 36-foot deposits in some regions. It has been calculated that the Tigris alone removes as much as 3 million tons of eroded highland materials in a single day. In the extreme south the two rivers join in a combined stream that today is known as the Shatt el-Arab.

The flooding of the Mesopotamian rivers in March and April differs from the Nile schedule which during that season is at its low ebb. The melting snows and rains at their sources create sudden, disastrous torrents that, along the Tigris especially, must be controlled by dams during such periods before they can supply a beneficial irrigation system. See Euphrates and Tigris Rivers.

The course of the Upper Euphrates was described as the northern border of the Promised Land (Gen. 15:18; Deut. 1:7; 11:24; Josh. 1:4). David, in fact, extended his military influence to its banks during the height of his power (2 Sam. 8:3; 10:16-18; 1 Kings 4:24). The terms "the river," "the flood," "the great river," and "beyond the river" (Josh. 24:2-3; Ezra 4:10-13; Neh. 2:7-9) refer to the Euphrates, historically a significant political and geographical boundary.

### 3. Tigris

From its source in a small lake (Hazar Golu), about 100 miles west of Lake Van, in Armenia, the Tigris flows in a southeasterly direction for about 1,150 miles before joining the Euphrates and emptying into the Persian Gulf. It achieves flood stage during March and April from the melting mountain snows and subsides after mid-May. While its upper flow is swift within narrow gorges, from Mosul and Nineveh southward its course was navigable and was extensively used in antiquity for transport. A series of tributaries from the slopes of the Zagros emptied into the Tigris from the east, including the Greater and Lesser Zab and the Diyala. The Diyala flows into the Tigris near Baghdad. In antiquity, its banks were inhabited by a dense population maintained and made prosperous by an excellent irrigation system. The Euphrates, flowing at a level nine meters higher than the Tigris, permitted the construction of a sequence of irrigation canals between the two rivers that resulted in unusual productivity. South of Baghdad where their courses again separated, a more complicated system of canals and diversions were necessary.

The banks of the Tigris were dotted by some of the most important cities of antiquity: Nineveh, the capital of Assyria during the Assyrian Empire; Asshur, the original capital of Assyria; Opis (in the vicinity of Baghdad), the important commercial center of Neo-Babylonian and later times; Ctesi-phon, the capital of the Parthians and Sassanians; and Seleucia, capital of the Seleucid rulers of Mesopotamia.
Rivers of Anatolia Several rivers water this part of modern Turkey. See Asia Minor.

### 4. Halys River

From its sources in the Armenian mountains, the Halys begins its 714-mile flow to the southwest only to be diverted by a secondary ridge into a broad loop until its direction is completely reversed into a northeasterly direction through the mountainous regions bordering the southern shore of the Black Sea. As the longest river in Anatolia, the Halys, like the other principal rivers in Turkey, is the result of heavy rainfall in the Pontic zone. Because of their winding courses within the coastal mountain chains, none of these rivers is navigable. Within this loop of the Halys in the northern Anatolian plateau the Hittites established their capital Boghazkoy. The course of the Halys generally formed the borders of the district of Pontus.

### 5. Rivers of the Aegean Coast

The broken Aegean coastline boasted a series of sheltered havens and inlets that prompted Greek colonization and the establishment the great harbor cities of the later Greek and Roman periods. The mouths of the Aegean rivers deemed ideal for maritime centers during colonization ultimately proved disastrous. The lower courses of these rivers, relatively short and following a meandering course over their respective plains, are very shallow and sluggish during the summer months. Their upper courses, however, of recent formation, carry enormous

quantities of alluvium from the highlands that tended to fill the estuaries and gulfs. Constant dredging was required to maintain the harbor's access to the sea and to avoid the formation of malaria-infested swamps. Thus the Hermus (155 miles) was diverted to prevent the destruction of the harbor of Smyrna (Izmir). To the south at Ephesus, the original townsite on the disease-ridden marshlands was abandoned about A.D. 400 for the construction of a new harbor on the Cayster River. During the days of Ephesus' prosperity, the constant dredging was adequately maintained. However, with the decline of the Roman Empire after A.D. 200, the silting of the harbor brought the rapid decline of the city. Miletus, on the alluvial plain of the Maeander River (236 miles), was originally established on a deep gulf well sheltered from the prevailing winds. The great Ionian city had possessed four harbors, but the silting of the harbors by the alluvial deposits of the Maeander ultimately brought about the decline and abandonment of the city. Though these Aegean rivers were not navigable, the alluvial plains that bordered them provided convenient and vital access and communications to the interior.
Rivers of Syro-Palestine In Syria and Palestine rivers often separated peoples rather than providing economic power.

## 6. Orontes and Litani

High within the Beqa valley that forms the rift between the Lebanon and Anti-Lebanon mountain ranges, a watershed (about 3,770 feet above sea level) forms the headwaters of the Orontes and Litani Rivers. The rains and snow on the mountain summits at heights of over 11,000 feet course down into the 6-10 mile-wide Beqa which is a part of the Great Rift ("Valley of Lebanon," Josh. 11:17). From the watershed, the Orontes flows northward and bends westward to empty into the Mediterranean near Antioch. The Litani flows southward and ultimately escapes to the sea north of Tyre. Unfortunately, its lower course has formed such a deep, narrow gorge that it is useless for communication. See Palestine.

## 7. Jordan River

A series of springs and tributaries, resulting from the rains and snows on the heights of Mount Hermon (up to 9,100 feet above sea level) at the southern end of the Anti-Lebanon mountains east of the Rift Valley, converge in Lake Huleh to form the headwaters of the Jordan River. Along the eastern edge of the Huleh Valley, it flows southward into Lake Kinnereth (the Sea of Galilee). Only about eight miles wide and fourteen miles long, the fresh waters of the Galilee and its fishing industry sustained a dense population during most historical periods. At the Galilee's southern end, the Jordan exits and flows 65 miles into the Dead Sea (about 1,300 feet below sea level). The Jordan flows 127 miles with a drainage area of about 6,380 square miles. The Yarmuk River joins the Jordan five miles south of the Sea of Galilee. The Jabbok River reaches the Jordan from the east twenty-five miles north of the Dead Sea.
At Jordan's end, the Dead Sea extends another 45 miles between high, rugged cliffs of Nubian sandstone and limestone between the arid wilderness bordering the Judean watershed on the west and the Transjordanian plateau on the east. The sea and the inhospitable terrain along its shoreline discouraged regular travel and transport within the area.

The Jordan appears never to have served as a waterway for travel or transport, but rather as a natural barrier and a political boundary, that because of its steep banks and the densely wooded fringe that lined its devious route ("thickets of the Jordan," Jer. 49:19, NIV; compare 2 Kings 6:4) could be crossed without difficulty only at its fords (Josh. 3). Control of the fords during military confrontations in biblical times constituted a critical advantage (Judg. 3:28; 12:5-6). The Jordan's role as a political boundary appears to have been established shortly after 2000 B.C. when the eastern frontier of the Egyptian province of Canaan followed the Jordan. Even though Israelite tribes were given special permission to settle in the Transjordan, it was always clear that, beyond the Jordan, they actually were residing outside the Promised Land (Josh 22). Even in postbiblical times, the eastern boundary of the Persian and Hellenistic province of Judea followed the Jordan. Apart from the fertile oases that dotted the Jordan Valley, agricultural prosperity was assured during the Hellenistic and Roman times when irrigation was developed along the gradual slopes on either side of the Jordan within the Rift Valley. See Jordan.

### 8. Kishon River

The Kishon River forms the drainage system of the Jezreel Plain and the southern portion of the Accho Plain. While a number of its small tributaries have their sources in springs at the base of Mount Tabor, in the southern Galilee, and in the extension of the Carmel in the vicinity of Taanach and Megiddo, the Kishon is rarely more than a brook within relatively shallow and narrow banks except during the heavy rains of the winter months. During those times its course becomes a marshy bog and impassable. From the Jezreel, it passes along the base of Mount Carmel through the narrow pass formed by a spur of the Galilean hills and into the Accho Plain, where some additional tributaries join before it empties into the Mediterranean. Its total length from the springs to the sea is only twenty-three miles. In biblical history, it is best known for its role in the Barak Deborah victory over the Canaanite forces of Sisera (Judg. 4-5) and Elijah's contest with the prophets of Baal on Mount Carmel (1 Kings 18:40).

### 9. Yarkon River

The Yarkon is formed by the seasonal runoff from the western slopes of the Samaritan and Judean hills that flows into the Brook Kanah, its major tributary, and the rich springs at the base of Aphek about eight miles inland from the Mediterranean shoreline. Though anchorages and small harbors, such as tel Qasile, a Philistine town, were established along its course and the cedar timbers from Lebanon were floated inland to Aphek for transport to Jerusalem for the construction of Solomon's palace and Temple, the Yarkon historically formed a major barrier to north-south traffic because of the extensive swamps that formed along its course. The profuse vegetation that bordered its banks probably suggested its name that was derived from the Hebrew yarok, meaning "green." The Yarkon, in biblical times, formed the border between the tribes of Dan and Ephraim to the north. Further inland, the Brook Kanah formed the boundary between Ephraim and Manasseh (Josh. 16:8; 17:9). George L. Kelm

## IV. Continuing with thoughts about the river

### A. The river can become a symbol of death Ex.1:22 KJV

*22 And Pharaoh charged all his people, saying, Every son that is born ye shall cast into the river, and every daughter ye shall save alive.*

**1.** The waters of baptism become death to the old man Rom. 6:1-6 KJV

**B. The river was used for washing and cleaning Ex. 2:5 KJV**

*5 And the daughter of Pharaoh came down to wash herself at the river; and her maidens walked along by the river's side; and when she saw the ark among the flags, she sent her maid to fetch it.*

**1. We are washed, cleansed by the Word of God Eph. 5:25-27 KJV**

*25 Husbands, love your wives, even as Christ also loved the church, and gave himself for it;*
*26 That he might sanctify and cleanse it with the washing of water by the word,*
*27 That he might present it to himself a glorious church, not having spot, or wrinkle, or any such thing; but that it should be holy and without blemish.*

**C. The river has many fish, which can be caught Ex. 7:18 KJV**

*18 And the fish that is in the river shall die, and the river shall stink; and the Egyptians shall loathe to drink of the water of the river.*

**Isa. 60:5** *Then thou shalt see, and flow together, and thine heart shall fear, and be enlarged; because the abundance of the sea shall be converted unto thee, the forces of the Gentiles shall come unto thee. KJV*

**D. Every person must have water in order to survive. The river can be a source of sustaining and refreshing Num. 21:5 KJV**

*5 And the people spake against God, and against Moses, Wherefore have ye brought us up out of Egypt to die in the wilderness? for there is no bread, neither is there any water; and our soul loatheth this light bread.*

**E. In the river comes a source of joy Ps. 46:4 KJV**

*4 There is a river, the streams whereof shall make glad the city of God, the holy place of the tabernacles of the most High.*

**F. The visitations of God come through the river Ps. 65:9 KJV**

*9 Thou visitest the earth, and waterest it: thou greatly enrichest it with the river of God, which is full of water: thou preparest them corn, when thou hast so provided for it.*

**G. The river comes from our Rock – even Christ Ps. 105:41 KJV**

*41 He opened the rock, and the waters gushed out; they ran in the dry places like a river.*

**1 Cor. 10:4** *And did all drink the same spiritual drink: for they drank of that spiritual Rock that followed them: and that Rock was Christ. KJV*

**John 15:26** *But when the Comforter is come, whom I will send unto you from the Father, even the Spirit of truth, which proceedeth from the Father, he shall testify of me: KJV*

**H. Our peace is to be like a flowing river Isa 66:12 KJV**

*12 For thus saith the LORD, Behold, I will extend peace to her like a river, and the glory of the Gentiles like a flowing stream: then shall ye suck, ye shall be borne upon her sides, and be dandled upon her knees.*

**I. The river brings life Ezek. 47:9 KJV**

*9 And it shall come to pass, that everything that liveth, which moveth, whithersoever the rivers shall come, shall live: and there shall be a very great multitude of fish, because these waters shall come thither: for they shall be healed; and everything shall live whither the river cometh.*

**Joel 3:18** *And it shall come to pass in that day, that the mountains shall drop down new wine, and the hills shall flow with milk, and all the rivers of Judah shall flow with waters, and a fountain shall come forth of the house of the LORD, and shall water the valley of Shittim. KJV*

**John 7:38** *He that believeth on me, as the scripture hath said, out of his belly shall flow rivers of living water. KJV*

**J. The river provides for healing Ezek. 47:12 KJV**

*12 And by the river upon the bank thereof, on this side and on that side, shall grow all trees for meat, whose leaf shall not fade, neither shall the fruit thereof be consumed: it shall bring forth new fruit according to his months, because their waters they issued out of the sanctuary: and the fruit thereof shall be for meat, and the leaf thereof for medicine.*

**Rev. 22:1-2 KJV**

*1 And he shewed me a pure river of water of life, clear as crystal, proceeding out of the throne of God and of the Lamb.*
*2 In the midst of the street of it, and on either side of the river, was there the tree of life, which bare twelve manner of fruits, and yielded her fruit every month: and the leaves of the tree were for the healing of the nations.*

**K. The river flows John 7:38-39 KJV**

*38 He that believeth on me, as the scripture hath said, out of his belly shall flow rivers of living water.*
*39(But this spake he of the Spirit, which they that believe on him should receive: for the Holy Ghost was not yet given; because that Jesus was not yet glorified.)*

1. **Flow** SC NT: a primary verb; to flow ("run"; as water)

**L. A river is not like a lake, pond, or ocean. It has constant motion. The scriptures tie the thought of a flowing river to the Holy Spirit. Because the river flows it is symbolic of the Holy Spirit's flow.**

1. When the church assembles – there is a flow from the beginning to the end. The worship and word will flow together in direction, purpose, and message.

2. The gifts of the Spirit in the service will flow in unity with the direction, purpose, and message of the day

**Ps. 147:16-18 KJV**

*16 He giveth snow like wool: he scattereth the hoarfrost like ashes.*
*17 He casteth forth his ice like morsels: who can stand before his cold?*
*18 He sendeth out his word, and melteth them: he causeth his wind to blow, and the waters flow.*

1. **Flow** SC OT: to drip, or shed by trickling

**Isa. 48:21** *And they thirsted not when he led them through the deserts: he caused the waters to flow out of the rock for them: he clave the rock also, and the waters gushed out. KJV*

**M. Joel prophesies about a time when the captives of Judah and Jerusalem will be rescued and restored. Note that part of the restoration is the flowing of the water Joel 3:18 KJV**

*18 And it shall come to pass in that day, that the mountains shall drop down new wine, and the hills shall flow with milk, and all the rivers of Judah shall flow with waters, and a fountain shall come forth of the house of the LORD, and shall water the valley of Shittim.*

1. **Flow** SC OT: a primitive root; to walk (literally or figuratively); causatively, to carry (in various senses)

   a. SC OT: to walk (in a great variety of applications, literally and figuratively)

**N. The spices of the bride are to flow so that the beloved can be a partaker Song 4:12-16 KJV**

*12 A garden inclosed is my sister, my spouse; a spring shut up, a fountain sealed.*
*13 Thy plants are an orchard of pomegranates, with pleasant fruits; camphire, with spikenard,*
*14 Spikenard and saffron; calamus and cinnamon, with all trees of frankincense; myrrh and aloes, with all the chief spices:*
*15 A fountain of gardens, a well of living waters, and streams from Lebanon.*
*16 Awake, O north wind; and come, thou south; blow upon my garden, that the spices thereof may flow out. Let my beloved come into his garden, and eat his pleasant fruits.*

**O. The nations are to flow into the church Isa. 2:2 KJV**

*2 And it shall come to pass in the last days, that the mountain of the LORD's house shall be established in the top of the mountains, and shall be exalted above the hills; and all nations shall flow unto it.*

**Isa. 60:1-5 KJV**

*1 Arise, shine; for thy light is come, and the glory of the LORD is risen upon thee.*

*2 For, behold, the darkness shall cover the earth, and gross darkness the people: but the LORD shall arise upon thee, and his glory shall be seen upon thee.*
*3 And the Gentiles shall come to thy light, and kings to the brightness of thy rising.*
*4 Lift up thine eyes round about, and see: all they gather themselves together, they come to thee: thy sons shall come from far, and thy daughters shall be nursed at thy side.*
*5 Then thou shalt see, and flow together, and thine heart shall fear, and be enlarged; because the abundance of the sea shall be converted unto thee, the forces of the Gentiles shall come unto thee.*

**Jer. 31:12** *Therefore they shall come and sing in the height of Zion, and shall flow together to the goodness of the LORD, for wheat, and for wine, and for oil, and for the young of the flock and of the herd: and their soul shall be as a watered garden; and they shall not sorrow any more at all. KJV*

**Mic. 4:1** *But in the last days it shall come to pass, that the mountain of the house of the LORD shall be established in the top of the mountains, and it shall be exalted above the hills; and people shall flow unto it. KJV*

# RAIN

## INTRO:

**The preceding chapter was the river, which the Word clearly states is the Holy Spirit. Now we will progress to water in the form of rain. There is not a single scripture with both words rain and the Holy Spirit contained within it. But, as you look at the whole of scripture you can find the tying together of rain and the Holy Spirit. For the purpose of this study I am using rain as a symbol of the Holy Spirit. The thought of rain is distinguishable but not inseparable from the Holy Spirit**

**Hos. 6:3** *Then shall we know, if we follow on to know the LORD: his going forth is prepared as the morning; and he shall come unto us as the rain, as the latter and former rain unto the earth. KJV*

**Ps. 72:6** *He shall come down like rain upon the mown grass: as showers that water the earth. KJV*

**Ps. 135:7** *He causeth the vapors to ascend from the ends of the earth; he maketh lightnings for the rain; he bringeth the wind out of his treasuries. KJV*

**Ps. 147:8** *Who covereth the heaven with clouds, who prepareth rain for the earth, who maketh grass to grow upon the mountains. KJV*

**Eccl. 11:3** *If the clouds be full of rain, they empty themselves upon the earth: and if the tree fall toward the south, or toward the north, in the place where the tree falleth, there it shall be. KJV*

I. **Rain is a symbol for more than one thing**

A. **Rain can be symbol of increase and fruitfulness Lev. 26:3-4 KJV**

*3 If ye walk in my statutes, and keep my commandments, and do them;*
*4 Then I will give you rain in due season, and the land shall yield her increase, and the trees of the field shall yield their fruit.*

B. **The promise land was cared for by the LORD. If the people obeyed His commandments rain was sent as the first and latter rains. This made the crops to grow and produce a harvest Deut. 11:10-17 KJV**

*10 For the land, whither thou goest in to possess it, is not as the land of Egypt, from whence ye came out, where thou sowedst thy seed, and wateredst it with thy foot, as a garden of herbs:*
*11 But the land, whither ye go to possess it, is a land of hills and valleys, and drinketh water of the rain of heaven:*
*12 A land which the LORD thy God careth for: the eyes of the LORD thy God are always upon it, from the beginning of the year even unto the end of the year.*
*13 And it shall come to pass, if ye shall hearken diligently unto my commandments which I command you this day, to love the LORD your God, and to serve him with all your heart and with all your soul,*
*14 That I will give you the rain of your land in his due season, the first rain and the latter rain, that thou mayest gather in thy corn, and thy wine, and thine oil.*
*15 And I will send grass in thy fields for thy cattle, that thou mayest eat and be full.*
*16 Take heed to yourselves, that your heart be not deceived, and ye turn aside, and serve other gods, and worship them;*
*17 And then the LORD's wrath be kindled against you, and he shut up the heaven, that there be no rain, and that the land yield not her fruit; and lest ye perish quickly from off the good land which the LORD giveth you.*

**C. The blessing of God on obedience resulted in treasure from heaven in the form of rain in its season. The workman was blessed to the point of lending unto many nations and not having to borrow Deut. 28:10-12 KJV**

*10 And all people of the earth shall see that thou art called by the name of the LORD; and they shall be afraid of thee.*
*11 And the LORD shall make thee plenteous in goods, in the fruit of thy body, and in the fruit of thy cattle, and in the fruit of thy ground, in the land which the LORD sware unto thy fathers to give thee.*
*12 The LORD shall open unto thee his good treasure, the heaven to give the rain unto thy land in his season, and to bless all the work of thine hand: and thou shalt lend unto many nations, and thou shalt not borrow.*

**D. Rain can speak of destruction and judgment Job 20:23 KJV**

*23 When he is about to fill his belly, God shall cast the fury of his wrath upon him, and shall rain it upon him while he is eating.*

**Ex. 9:18** *Behold, tomorrow about this time I will cause it to rain a very grievous hail, such as hath not been in Egypt since the foundation thereof even until now. KJV*

**Isa. 4:6** *And there shall be a tabernacle for a shadow in the daytime from the heat, and for a place of refuge, and for a covert from storm and from rain. KJV*

1. **Covert** SC OT: a refuge

   a. SC OT: to hide (by covering), literally or figuratively

**E. Rain is a symbol of Doctrine or the Word of God - doctrine shall drop as rain Deut. 32:2 KJV**

*2 My doctrine shall drop as the rain, my speech shall distill as the dew, as the small rain upon the tender herb, and as the showers upon the grass:*

1. **Drop** SC OT: to droop; hence, to drip

**Isa. 55:10-11 KJV**

*10 For as the rain cometh down, and the snow from heaven, and returneth not thither, but watereth the earth, and maketh it bring forth and bud, that it may give seed to the sower, and bread to the eater:*
*11 So shall my word be that goeth forth out of my mouth: it shall not return unto me void, but it shall accomplish that which I please, and it shall prosper in the thing whereto I sent it.*

**II. The prophet Joel prophecies about the former and latter rains followed by the pouring out of the Holy Spirit in Joel 2:23-28 KJV. Rain becomes a symbol of the Holy Spirit.**

*23 Be glad then, ye children of Zion, and rejoice in the LORD your God: for he hath given you the former rain moderately, and he will cause to come down for you the rain, the former rain, and the latter rain in the first month.*
*24 And the floors shall be full of wheat, and the fats shall overflow with wine and oil.*
*25 And I will restore to you the years that the locust hath eaten, the cankerworm, and the caterpiller, and the palmerworm, my great army which I sent among you.*
*26 And ye shall eat in plenty, and be satisfied, and praise the name of the LORD your God, that hath dealt wondrously with you: and my people shall never be ashamed.*
*27 And ye shall know that I am in the midst of Israel, and that I am the LORD your God, and none else: and my people shall never be ashamed.*
*28 And it shall come to pass afterward, that I will pour out my spirit upon all flesh; and your sons and your daughters shall prophesy, your old men shall dream dreams, your young men shall see visions:*

**A. It is the work of the Holy Spirit to convict a person of sin. He prepares the heart with conviction so when the seed is sown it will find a lodging place in the heart John 16:7-9 AMP**

*7 However, I am telling you nothing but the truth when I say it is profitable (good, expedient, advantageous) for you that I go away. Because if I do not go away, the Comforter (Counselor, Helper, Advocate, Intercessor, Strengthener, Standby) will not come to you [into close fellowship with you]; but if I go away, I will send Him to you [to be in close fellowship with you].*
*8 And when He comes, He will convict and convince the world and bring demonstration to it about sin and about righteousness (uprightness of heart and right standing with God) and about judgment:*
*9 About sin, because they do not believe in Me [trust in, rely on, and adhere to Me];*

**B. The early rain prepared the soil for the planting of the seed – the Word of God Luke 8:9-11 KJV**

*9 And his disciples asked him, saying, What might this parable be?*
*10 And he said, Unto you it is given to know the mysteries of the kingdom of God: but to others in parables; that seeing they might not see, and hearing they might not understand.*
*11 Now the parable is this: The seed is the word of God.*

**III. International Standard Bible Encyclopedia RAIN**

The "former rains" are the showers of October and the first part of November. They soften the parched ground so that the winter grain may be sown before the heavy continuous rains set in. The main bulk of the rain falls in the months of December, January and February. Although in these months the rains are frequent and heavy, a dark, foggy day is seldom seen. The "latter rains" of April are the most highly appreciated, because they ripen the fruit and stay the drought of summer. They were considered a special blessing: Yahweh "will come .... as the latter rain that watereth the earth" (Hos. 6:3); "They opened their mouth wide as for the latter rain" (Job 29:23); and as a reason for worshipping Yahweh who sent them, "Let us now fear Yahweh our God, that giveth rain, both the former and the latter, in its season" (Jer. 5:24).

## IV. McClintock and Strong Encyclopedia RAIN

Disadvantages occasioned by this long absence of rain: the whole land becomes dry, parched, and brown; the cisterns are empty; the springs and fountains fail; and the autumnal rains are eagerly looked for, to prepare the earth for the reception of the seed. These, the early rains, commence about the end of October or beginning of November, in Lebanon a month earlier not suddenly, but by degrees: the husbandman has thus the opportunity of sowing his fields of wheat and barley.

Rain continues to fall more or less during the month of March; it is very rare in April, and even in Lebanon the showers that occur are generally light. In the valley of the Jordan the barley harvest begins as early as the middle of April, and the wheat a fortnight later; in Lebanon the grain is seldom ripe before the middle of June.

## V. Nelson's Illustrated Bible Dictionary RAIN

1. Rain is often a symbol of abundance in the Bible, further testimony to the occasional heaviness of Palestine's rain. This abundance is compared with the effectiveness of God's Word Deut. 32:2; Isa. 55:10

2. With the righteousness and peace of God's kingdom Ps. 72:6-7; Hos. 10:12

3. With God's provision of food in the wilderness Ex. 16:4; Ps. 78:24, 27

4. But rain could also be destructive Prov. 28:3; Isa. 4:6

5. The Bible sometimes speaks of the rain as a sign of God's judgment, when He might rain down hail, fire, or brimstone Ex. 9:18

## VI. The New Unger's Bible Dictionary RAIN

**Figurative.** Rain frequently furnishes the writers of the OT with forcible and appropriate metaphors:

1. Of the word of God (Isa. 55:10); as rain and snow return as vapor to the sky, but not without having, first of all, accomplished the purpose of their descent, so the word of God shall not return to Him without fulfilling its purpose.

2. The wise and refreshing doctrine of faithful ministers Deut. 32:2; Job 29:23

3. Of Christ in the communications of His grace 2 Sam. 23:4; Ps. 72:6; 84:6; Ezek. 34:26; Hos. 6:3

4. Destructive, God's judgments Job 20:23; Ps 11:6; Ezek. 38:22, of a poor man oppressing the poor Prov. 28:3

## VII. The former and the latter rains

### A. Early Rain means the rains of the autumn

1. **Months:** Mid October to mid-December (October-November)

2. **Purpose:** The ground was very dry and parched with the long dry season. The early rains softened the ground for plowing and sowing. The seed was planted when the early rains came.

3. The concordance defines the latter rain as follows: It defines the rain as teaching

   a. **The former rain** SC OT: an archer; also teacher or teaching; also the early rain

   b. SC OT: to flow as water (i.e. to rain); transitively, to lay or throw (especially an arrow, i.e. to shoot); figuratively, to point out (as if by aiming the finger), to teach

   c. SC OT: sprinkling; hence, a sprinkling (or autumnal showers)

### B. The latter rains

1. **Months:** February-March

2. **Purpose:** The "latter rains" of April ripen the crop and stay the drought of summer. These rains prepare for the harvest of the crop

3. **The concordance defines the latter rain as follows: the spring rain, to gather the after crop**

   a. **The Latter Rain** SC OT: the spring rain

   b. SC OT: to gather the after crop

## VIII. Jamieson, Fausset, and Brown Commentary Joel 2:21-23

For he hath given you the former rain moderately, and he will cause to come down for you the rain, the former rain, and the latter rain. The autumnal, or "former rain," from the middle of October to the middle of December, is put first, as Joel prophesies in summer, when the locusts' invasion took place, and therefore looks to the time of early sowing in autumn, when the autumnal rain was indispensably required. Next, "the rain," generically [geshem (OT: 1653)], literally, the showering or heavy rain. Next, the two species of the latter. "the former and the latter rain" (in March and April). The repetition of "the former rain" implies that He will give it not merely for the exigence of that particular season when Joel spake, but also for the future in the regular course of nature, the autumn and the spring rain; the former being put first, in the order of nature, as being required for the sowing in autumn, as the latter is required in, spring for maturing the young crop. The margin, 'a teacher of righteousness' [hamowreh (OT: 4175) litsdaaqaah (OT: 6666)], instead of "the former rain moderately," literally, 'according to righteousness,' has against it the objection that the same Hebrew word is translated "former rain" in the next sentence, and cannot therefore be differently translated here. Besides, Joel begins with the inferior and temporal blessings, and not until Joel 2:28 proceeds to the higher and spiritual ones, of which the former are the pledge.

Moderately - rather, 'in due measure,' as much, as the land requires-literally, 'according to right;' neither too much nor too little, either of which extremes would hurt the crop (cf. Deut. 11:14; Prov.16:15; Jer. 5:24; note, Hos. 6:3). The phrase, 'in due measure,' in this clause, is parallel to 'in the first month,' in the last clause (i.e., 'in the month when first it is needed,' each rain in its proper season). Or else, "as at the first" (Isa. 1:26; Hos. 2:15; Mal. 3:4). Heretofore the just or right order of nature has been interrupted through your sin; now God will restore it. Pusey, however, gives the following reasons for translating 'for He giveth you (or will give you) the Teacher unto righteousness' (i.e., the object of whose coming is righteousness; who brings in everlasting righteousness), (Dan. 9.)

**The early rain prepared the soil to receive the seed, the word**
**The latter rain matured the crop for harvest**

## IX. Man's disobedience and sin has a direct effect on the abundance of rain 1 Kings 8:35-36 KJV

*35 When heaven is shut up, and there is no rain, because they have sinned against thee; if they pray toward this place, and confess thy name, and turn from their sin, when thou afflictest them:*
*36 Then hear thou in heaven, and forgive the sin of thy servants, and of thy people Israel, that thou teach them the good way wherein they should walk, and give rain upon thy land, which thou hast given to thy people for an inheritance.*

### A. When the people prayed and repented, rain, the blessing of heaven was poured out 2 Chr. 6:27 KJV

*27 Then hear thou from heaven, and forgive the sin of thy servants, and of thy people Israel, when thou hast taught them the good way, wherein they should walk; and send rain upon thy land, which thou hast given unto thy people for an inheritance.*

**Hos 6:1-3 KJV**

*1 Come, and let us return unto the LORD: for he hath torn, and he will heal us; he hath smitten, and he will bind us up.*
*2 After two days will he revive us: in the third day he will raise us up, and we shall live in his sight.*
*3 Then shall we know, if we follow on to know the LORD: his going forth is prepared as the morning; and he shall come unto us as the rain, as the latter and former rain unto the earth.*

# WATER

## INTRO:

**Jesus declared that out of the believer's innermost being would flow rivers of living WATER. Jesus was speaking about the Holy Spirit John 7:37-39 KJV**

*37 In the last day, that great day of the feast, Jesus stood and cried, saying, If any man thirst, let him come unto me, and drink.*
*38 He that believeth on me, as the scripture hath said, out of his belly shall flow rivers of living water.*
*39(But this spake he of the Spirit, which they that believe on him should receive: for the Holy Ghost was not yet given; because that Jesus was not yet glorified.)*

**Isa. 44:3** *For I will pour water upon him that is thirsty, and floods upon the dry ground: I will pour my spirit upon thy seed, and my blessing upon thine offspring: KJV*

**Once again water and the Holy Spirit are tied together – another symbol of the Holy Spirit**

**I. There are many purposes for water – each truth reveals a work of the Holy Spirit in a person's life.**

**A. Water is used to sanctify and cleanse the Church – The Holy Spirit washes us through the Word of God Eph. 5:25-26 KJV**

*25 Husbands, love your wives, even as Christ also loved the church, and gave himself for it;*
*26 That he might sanctify and cleanse it with the washing of water by the word,*

1. **Sanctify** SC NT: to make holy, i.e. (ceremonially) purify or consecrate; (mentally) to venerate

    a. **Thayers Greek Lexicon**

    1. To render or acknowledge, or to be venerable or to hallow

    2. To separate from profane things and to dedicate to God

    a. To consecrate things to God

**b.** To dedicate people to God

**3.** To purify

**a.** To cleanse externally

**b.** To purify by expiation: to free from the guilt of sin

**c.** To purify internally by a renewing of the soul

**2.** **Cleanse** SC NT: to cleanse (literally or figuratively)

**a.** **Thayers Greek Lexicon**

**1.** To make clean, to cleanse

**a.** From physical stains and dirt or disease

**1.** Utensils, food

**2.** To cleanse a leper by curing him

**3.** To remove by cleansing

**b.** In a moral sense

**1.** To free from defilement of sin and from faults

**2.** To purify from wickedness

**3.** To free from guilt of sin, to purify

**4.** To consecrate by cleansing or purifying

**5.** To consecrate, dedicate

**2.** To pronounce clean in a Levitical sense

**3.** **Washing** SC NT: a bath, i.e. (figuratively), immersion, baptism

**B.** **Water was used in cleansing the leper Lev. 14:8 KJV**

*8 And he that is to be cleansed shall wash his clothes, and shave off all his hair, and wash himself in water, that he may be clean: and after that he shall come into the camp, and shall tarry abroad out of his tent seven days.*

**Lev. 14:51-52 KJV**

*51 And he shall take the cedar wood, and the hyssop, and the scarlet, and the living bird, and dip them in the blood of the slain bird, and in the running water, and sprinkle the house seven times:*

*52 And he shall cleanse the house with the blood of the bird, and with the running water, and with the living bird, and with the cedar wood, and with the hyssop, and with the scarlet:*

1. **Cleanse** SC OT: to miss; hence (figuratively and generally) to sin; by inference, to forfeit, lack, expiate, repent, (causatively) lead astray, condemn

2. **Thayer's Greek Lexicon**

    a. To make clean, to cleanse

        1. From physical stains and dirt: e. g. utensils, Matt. 23:25, Matt. 23:26; Luke 11:39; food, Mark 7:19

        2. A leper, to cleanse by curing, Matt. 8:2f; 10:8; 11:5; Mark 1:40-42; Luke 4:27; 5:12 f; 7:22; 17:14, 17 (Lev. 14:8)

        3. To remove by cleansing: Matt. 8:3, Deut. 19:13

            a. The custom of marrying heathen women, Josephus (75 A.D.), Antiquities 11, 5, 4; Homer (900 B.C.?), Iliad 16, 667

            b. In a moral sense; to free from the defilement of sin and from faults; to purify from wickedness: 2 Cor. 7:1; Acts 15:9

            c. To abstain in future from wrong-doing, James 4:8

        4. To free from the guilt of sin, to purify 1 John 1:7; 1 John 1:9)

        5. To consecrate by cleansing or purifying Heb. 9:22

C. **Running Water is used in cleansing Lev. 14:51-52 KJV**

*51 And he shall take the cedar wood, and the hyssop, and the scarlet, and the living bird, and dip them in the blood of the slain bird, and in the running water, and sprinkle the house seven times:*

*52 And he shall cleanse the house with the blood of the bird, and with the running water, and with the living bird, and with the cedar wood, and with the hyssop, and with the scarlet:*

1. **Rinsing in water is also part of cleansing Lev. 6:28 KJV**

*28 But the earthen vessel wherein it is sodden shall be broken: and if it be sodden in a brazen pot, it shall be both scoured, and rinsed in water.*

**D. In the dry and barren seasons of life water is given to start the process of new life – it will bring hope and a new progression Job 14:7-9 KJV**

*7 For there is hope of a tree, if it be cut down, that it will sprout again, and that the tender branch thereof will not cease.*
*8 Though the root thereof wax old in the earth, and the stock thereof die in the ground;*
*9 Yet through the scent of water it will bud, and bring forth boughs like a plant.*

**Isa. 41:17-18 KJV**

*17 When the poor and needy seek water, and there is none, and their tongue faileth for thirst, I the LORD will hear them, I the God of Israel will not forsake them.*
*18 I will open rivers in high places, and fountains in the midst of the valleys: I will make the wilderness a pool of water, and the dry land springs of water.*

**E. During the times of restoration fresh water will flow. Joel 3:18 KJV**

*18 And it shall come to pass in that day, that the mountains shall drop down new wine, and the hills shall flow with milk, and all the rivers of Judah shall flow with waters, and a fountain shall come forth of the house of the LORD, and shall water the valley of Shittim.*

**F. Rain softens the hard dry parched ground – a hardened heart Isa. 35:4-10 KJV**

*4 Say to them that are of a fearful heart, Be strong, fear not: behold, your God will come with vengeance, even God with a recompense; he will come and save you.*
*5 Then the eyes of the blind shall be opened, and the ears of the deaf shall be unstopped.*
*6 Then shall the lame man leap as an hart, and the tongue of the dumb sing: for in the wilderness shall waters break out, and streams in the desert.*
*7 And the parched ground shall become a pool, and the thirsty land springs of water: in the habitation of dragons, where each lay, shall be grass with reeds and rushes.*
*8 And an highway shall be there, and a way, and it shall be called The way of holiness; the unclean shall not pass over it; but it shall be for those: the wayfaring men, though fools, shall not err therein.*
*9 No lion shall be there, nor any ravenous beast shall go up thereon, it shall not be found there; but the redeemed shall walk there:*
*10 And the ransomed of the LORD shall return, and come to Zion with songs and everlasting joy upon their heads: they shall obtain joy and gladness, and sorrow and sighing shall flee away.*

**G. Fruitfulness is produced because of the rain Joel 2:23-24 KJV**

*23 Be glad then, ye children of Zion, and rejoice in the LORD your God: for he hath given you the former rain moderately, and he will cause to come down for you the rain, the former rain, and the latter rain in the first month.*
*24 And the floors shall be full of wheat, and the fats shall overflow with wine and oil.*

**H. Water is essential for sustaining life – everyone needs a good drink of water Prov. 25:25 KJV**

*25 As cold waters to a thirsty soul, so is good news from a far country.*

**I. Water satisfies a thirsting soul – Salvation brings lifelong desires to pass John 4:13-14 KJV**

*13 Jesus answered and said unto her, Whosoever drinketh of this water shall thirst again:*
*14 But whosoever drinketh of the water that I shall give him shall never thirst; but the water that I shall give him shall be in him a well of water springing up into everlasting life.*

**J. The pleasures of God are like a river of water Ps. 36:8 KJV**

*8 They shall be abundantly satisfied with the fatness of thy house; and thou shalt make them drink of the river of thy pleasures.*

1. **Pleasures** SC OT: pleasure

**K. Water causes us to be glad or brighten up Ps. 46:4 KJV**

*4 There is a river, the streams whereof shall make glad the city of God, the holy place of the tabernacles of the most High.*

1. **Glad** SC OT: probably to brighten up, i.e. (figuratively) be (causatively, make) blithe or gleesome

**L. Water is the sustainer of life Ex. 17:1-6 KJV**

*1 And all the congregation of the children of Israel journeyed from the wilderness of Sin, after their journeys, according to the commandment of the LORD, and pitched in Rephidim: and there was no water for the people to drink.*
*2 Wherefore the people did chide with Moses, and said, Give us water that we may drink. And Moses said unto them, Why chide ye with me? Wherefore do ye tempt the LORD?*
*3 And the people thirsted there for water; and the people murmured against Moses, and said, Wherefore is this that thou hast brought us up out of Egypt, to kill us and our children and our cattle with thirst?*
*4 And Moses cried unto the LORD, saying, What shall I do unto this people? They be almost ready to stone me.*
*5 And the LORD said unto Moses, Go on before the people, and take with thee of the elders of Israel; and thy rod, wherewith thou smotest the river, take in thine hand, and go.*
*6 Behold, I will stand before thee there upon the rock in Horeb; and thou shalt smite the rock, and there shall come water out of it, that the people may drink. And Moses did so in the sight of the elders of Israel.*

**M. Waters are symbolic of humanity Isa. 8:7 KJV**

*7 Now therefore, behold, the Lord bringeth up upon them the waters of the river, strong and many, even the king of Assyria, and all his glory: and he shall come up over all his channels, and go over all his banks:*

**Rev. 17:1 & 15 KJV**

*1 And there came one of the seven angels which had the seven vials, and talked with me, saying unto me, Come hither; I will shew unto thee the judgment of the great whore that sitteth upon many waters:*

*15 And he saith unto me, The waters which thou sawest, where the whore sitteth, are peoples, and multitudes, and nations, and tongues.*

**N. Water also speaks of affliction Ps. 69:1-2 KJV**

*1 Save me, O God; for the waters are come in unto my soul.*
*2 I sink in deep mire, where there is no standing: I am come into deep waters, where the floods overflow me.*

**Isa. 30:20** *And though the Lord give you the bread of adversity, and the water of affliction, yet shall not thy teachers be removed into a corner anymore, but thine eyes shall see thy teachers: KJV*

**Isa. 43:1-2 KJV**

*1 But now thus saith the LORD that created thee, O Jacob, and he that formed thee, O Israel, Fear not: for I have redeemed thee, I have called thee by thy name; thou art mine.*
*2 When thou passest through the waters, I will be with thee; and through the rivers, they shall not overflow thee: when thou walkest through the fire, thou shalt not be burned; neither shall the flame kindle upon thee.*

**II. Our salvation experience involves a drink of fresh living water from the wells of salvation. This experience provides eternal life, satisfaction, and the beginning of fulfilling life-long desires Isa. 12:3 KJV**

*3 Therefore with joy shall ye draw water out of the wells of salvation.*

a. **Wells** SC OT: a denominative in the sense of a spring); a fountain (also collectively), figuratively, a source (of satisfaction)

**John 4:10-14 KJV**

*10 Jesus answered and said unto her, If thou knewest the gift of God, and who it is that saith to thee, Give me to drink; thou wouldest have asked of him, and he would have given thee living water.*
*11 The woman saith unto him, Sir, thou hast nothing to draw with, and the well is deep: from whence then hast thou that living water?*
*12 Art thou greater than our father Jacob, which gave us the well, and drank thereof himself, and his children, and his cattle?*
*13 Jesus answered and said unto her, Whosoever drinketh of this water shall thirst again:*
*14 But whosoever drinketh of the water that I shall give him shall never thirst; but the water that I shall give him shall be in him a well of water springing up into everlasting life.*

**Joel 3:18** *And it shall come to pass in that day, that the mountains shall drop down new wine, and the hills shall flow with milk, and all the rivers of Judah shall flow with waters, and a fountain shall come forth of the house of the LORD, and shall water the valley of Shittim. KJV*

**Zech. 13:1** *In that day there shall be a fountain opened to the house of David and to the inhabitants of Jerusalem for sin and for uncleanness. KJV*

**Rev. 21:6** *And he said unto me, It is done. I am Alpha and Omega, the beginning and the end. I will give unto him that is athirst of the fountain of the water of life freely. KJV*

A. **To drink of the water of the wells of salvation will result in joy**

**Ps. 51:12** *Restore unto me the joy of thy salvation; and uphold me with thy free spirit. KJV*

**Ps. 16:11** *Thou wilt shew me the path of life: in thy presence is fullness of joy; at thy right hand there are pleasures for evermore. KJV*

**Ps. 27:6** *And now shall mine head be lifted up above mine enemies round about me: therefore will I offer in his tabernacle sacrifices of joy; I will sing, yea, I will sing praises unto the LORD. KJV*

**Ps. 132:16** *I will also clothe her priests with salvation: and her saints shall shout aloud for joy. KJV*

**Isa. 35:10** *And the ransomed of the LORD shall return, and come to Zion with songs and everlasting joy upon their heads: they shall obtain joy and gladness, and sorrow and sighing shall flee away. KJV*

**Isa. 61:3** *To appoint unto them that mourn in Zion, to give unto them beauty for ashes, the oil of joy for mourning, the garment of praise for the spirit of heaviness; that they might be called trees of righteousness, the planting of the LORD, that he might be glorified. KJV*

**Neh. 8:10** *Then he said unto them, Go your way, eat the fat, and drink the sweet, and send portions unto them for whom nothing is prepared: for this day is holy unto our Lord: neither be ye sorry; for the joy of the LORD is your strength. KJV*

B. **Moses smote the rock and water came forth – the rock was Christ. To drink from the rock was to have a spiritual drink Ex. 17:6 KJV**

*6 Behold, I will stand before thee there upon the rock in Horeb; and thou shalt smite the rock, and there shall come water out of it, that the people may drink. And Moses did so in the sight of the elders of Israel.*

**1 Cor. 10:4** *And did all drink the same spiritual drink: for they drank of that spiritual Rock that followed them: and that Rock was Christ. KJV*

**C. Water baptism is an integral part of our salvation experience – it speaks of death and separation Rom. 6:3-6 KJV**

*3 Know ye not, that so many of us as were baptized into Jesus Christ were baptized into his death?*
*4 Therefore we are buried with him by baptism into death: that like as Christ was raised up from the dead by the glory of the Father, even so we also should walk in newness of life.*
*5 For if we have been planted together in the likeness of his death, we shall be also in the likeness of his resurrection:*
*6 Knowing this, that our old man is crucified with him, that the body of sin might be destroyed, that henceforth we should not serve sin.*

**1. John the Baptist baptized with water – a baptism of repentance Matt. 3:11 KJV**

*11 I indeed baptize you with water unto repentance: but he that cometh after me is mightier than I, whose shoes I am not worthy to bear: he shall baptize you with the Holy Ghost, and with fire:*

**III. The properties of water**

**A. Water takes the shape of the container that it resides in – The Holy Spirit is at home in each believer's body. Regardless of age, size, sex, or ethnic group – He resides in us! John 14:23 KJV**

*23 Jesus answered and said unto him, If a man love me, he will keep my words: and my Father will love him, and we will come unto him, and make our abode with him.*

**1. Abode** SC NT: a staying, i.e. residence (the act or the place)

**a.** SC NT: a primary verb; to stay (in a given place, state, relation or expectancy)

**John 14:16** *And I will pray the Father, and he shall give you another Comforter, that he may abide with you forever; KJV*

**1. Abide** SC NT: I exist

**1 Cor. 6:19** *What? know ye not that your body is the temple of the Holy Ghost which is in you, which ye have of God, and ye are not your own? KJV*

**1 Cor. 3:16** *Know ye not that ye are the temple of God, and that the Spirit of God dwelleth in you? KJV*

**1. Dwelleth** SC NT: to occupy a house, i.e. reside (figuratively, inhabit, remain, in here); by implication to cohabit

**a.** SC NT: a dwelling (more or less extensive, literal or figurative); by implication a family (more or less related, literal or figuratively)

**B. Water has the property of change – the Holy Spirit can operate in any given situation**

1. A solid state or frozen — Job 38:30
2. A gas state or vapor — Job 36:27
3. A liquid state — Lev. 14:15

**C. Water has the ability to carry dirt, debris, or anything**

**D. Water has the ability to take stones that are rough and make them smooth**

**E. Water has the ability to cut new channels** – a river overflowing its banks will make new channels to flow in

**F. Water has the ability to sustain life** – human, animals, plants, all sea life

**G. Water has the ability to be a liquid and solid-state at the same time** - snow/rain mix

**H. Water can become stagnant if it is not flowing** – the life-giving water becomes detrimental to living creatures

# FIRE

## INTRO:

**The fifth symbol of the Holy Spirit is Fire Matt. 3:11 KJV**

*11 I indeed baptize you with water unto repentance: but he that cometh after me is mightier than I, whose shoes I am not worthy to bear: he shall baptize you with the Holy Ghost, and with fire:*

**Luke 3:16-17 KJV**

*16 John answered, saying unto them all, I indeed baptize you with water; but one mightier than I cometh, the latchet of whose shoes I am not worthy to unloose: he shall baptize you with the Holy Ghost and with fire:*

*17 Whose fan is in his hand, and he will thoroughly purge his floor, and will gather the wheat into his garner; but the chaff he will burn with fire unquenchable.*

**I. Fire is associated with being filled with the Spirit Acts 2:1-5 KJV**

*1 And when the day of Pentecost was fully come, they were all with one accord in one place.*

*2 And suddenly there came a sound from heaven as of a rushing mighty wind, and it filled all the house where they were sitting.*

*3 And there appeared unto them cloven tongues like as of fire, and it sat upon each of them.*

*4 And they were all filled with the Holy Ghost, and began to speak with other tongues, as the Spirit gave them utterance.*

1. **Fire** SC NT: fire literally or figuratively, specifically, lightening

**II. A revelation of God is that He is a consuming fire**

**Deut. 4:24** *For the LORD thy God is a consuming fire, even a jealous God. KJV*

**Heb. 12:29** *For our God is a consuming fire. KJV*

**A. Throughout the history of Israel God would appear with fire**

1. **Moses experienced a burning bush that was not consumed Ex. 3:2 KJV**

*2 And the angel of the LORD appeared unto him in a flame of fire out of the midst of a bush: and he looked, and, behold, the bush burned with fire, and the bush was not consumed.*

**2. The children of Israel experienced the fire of God as protection Ex. 13:21-22 KJV**

*21 And the LORD went before them by day in a pillar of a cloud, to lead them the way; and by night in a pillar of fire, to give them light; to go by day and night:*
*22 He took not away the pillar of the cloud by day, nor the pillar of fire by night, from before the people.*

**3. God descended upon Mount Sinai in fire Ex. 19:18 KJV**

*18 And mount Sinai was altogether on a smoke, because the LORD descended upon it in fire: and the smoke thereof ascended as the smoke of a furnace, and the whole mount quaked greatly.*

**Ex. 24:17** *And the sight of the glory of the LORD was like devouring fire on the top of the mount in the eyes of the children of Israel. KJV*

**4. Elijah was used by God to turn the hearts of Israel back to God by establishing an altar with a sacrifice – the fire of God fell upon the sacrifice and consumed it 1 Kings 18:19-24 KJV**

*19 Now therefore send, and gather to me all Israel unto mount Carmel, and the prophets of Baal four hundred and fifty, and the prophets of the groves four hundred, which eat at Jezebel's table.*
*20 So Ahab sent unto all the children of Israel, and gathered the prophets together unto mount Carmel.*
*21 And Elijah came unto all the people, and said, How long halt ye between two opinions? if the LORD be God, follow him: but if Baal, then follow him. And the people answered him not a word.*
*22 Then said Elijah unto the people, I, even I only, remain a prophet of the LORD; but Baal's prophets are four hundred and fifty men.*
*23 Let them therefore give us two bullocks; and let them choose one bullock for themselves, and cut it in pieces, and lay it on wood, and put no fire under: and I will dress the other bullock, and lay it on wood, and put no fire under:*
*24 And call ye on the name of your gods, and I will call on the name of the LORD: and the God that answereth by fire, let him be God. And all the people answered and said, It is well-spoken.*

**1 Kings 18:36-39 KJV**
*36 And it came to pass at the time of the offering of the evening sacrifice, that Elijah the prophet came near, and said, LORD God of Abraham, Isaac, and of Israel, let it be known this day that thou art God in Israël, and that I am thy servant, and that I have done all these things at thy word.*
*37 Hear me, O LORD, hear me, that this people may know that thou art the LORD God, and that thou hast turned their heart back again.*
*38 Then the fire of the LORD fell, and consumed the burnt sacrifice, and the wood, and the stones, and the dust, and licked up the water that was in the trench.*
*39 And when all the people saw it, they fell on their faces: and they said, The LORD, he is the God; the LORD, he is the God.*

**III. Sacrifices were established and offered upon an altar. These were burnt offerings that the sons of Aaron the high priest placed on the brazen altar Lev. 1:7-8 KJV**

*7 And the sons of Aaron the priest shall put fire upon the altar, and lay the wood in order upon the fire:*
*8 And the priests, Aaron's sons, shall lay the parts, the head, and the fat, in order upon the wood that is on the fire which is upon the altar:*

**Ex. 29:18** *And thou shalt burn the whole ram upon the altar: it is a burnt offering unto the LORD: it is a sweet savour, an offering made by fire unto the LORD. KJV*

**A. Their sacrifices involved fire. Note the sacrifices of the believer:**

**1. The sacrifice of praise Heb. 13:15 KJV**

*15 By him therefore let us offer the sacrifice of praise to God continually, that is, the fruit of our lips giving thanks to his name.*

**Ps. 54:6** *I will freely sacrifice unto thee: I will praise thy name, O LORD; for it is good. KJV*

**Jer. 33:11** *The voice of joy, and the voice of gladness, the voice of the bridegroom, and the voice of the bride, the voice of them that shall say, Praise the LORD of hosts: for the LORD is good; for his mercy endureth forever: and of them that shall bring the sacrifice of praise into the house of the LORD. For I will cause to return the captivity of the land, as at the first, saith the LORD. KJV*

**2. The sacrifice of thanksgiving Ps. 107:21-22 KJV**

*21 Oh that men would praise the LORD for his goodness, and for his wonderful works to the children of men!*
*22 And let them sacrifice the sacrifices of thanksgiving, and declare his works with rejoicing.*

**Ps. 116:17** *I will offer to thee the sacrifice of thanksgiving, and will call upon the name of the LORD. KJV*

**3. The sacrifice of your body Rom. 12:1 KJV**

*1 I beseech you therefore, brethren, by the mercies of God, that ye present your bodies a living sacrifice, holy, acceptable unto God, which is your reasonable service.*

**4. The sacrifice of a broken and contrite heart Ps. 51:16-17 KJV**

*16 For thou desirest not sacrifice; else would I give it: thou delightest not in burnt offering.*
*17 The sacrifices of God are a broken spirit: a broken and a contrite heart, O God, thou wilt not despise.*

**5. The sacrifice of joy Ps. 27:6 KJV**

*6 And now shall mine head be lifted up above mine enemies round about me: therefore will I offer in his tabernacle sacrifices of joy; I will sing, yea, I will sing praises unto the LORD.*

### 6. Obedience and sacrifice are joined in 1 Sam. 15:22-23 KJV

*22 And Samuel said, Hath the LORD as great delight in burnt offerings and sacrifices, as in obeying the voice of the LORD? Behold, to obey is better than sacrifice, and to hearken than the fat of rams.*
*23 For rebellion is as the sin of witchcraft, and stubbornness is as iniquity and idolatry. Because thou hast rejected the word of the LORD, he hath also rejected thee from being king.*

**Ps. 40:6-8 KJV**
*6 Sacrifice and offering thou didst not desire; mine ears hast thou opened: burnt offering and sin offering hast thou not required.*
*7 Then said I, Lo, I come: in the volume of the book it is written of me,*
*8 I delight to do thy will, O my God: yea, thy law is within my heart.*

### 7. The sacrifices of giving Phil. 4:18 KJV

*18 But I have all, and abound: I am full, having received of Epaphroditus the things which were sent from you, an odour of a sweet smell, a sacrifice acceptable, well pleasing to God.*

## IV. The trials that come to the believer are as fire

### A. The trial of your faith I Pet. 1:7 KJV

*7 That the trial of your faith, being much more precious than of gold that perisheth, though it be tried with fire, might be found unto praise and honour and glory at the appearing of Jesus Christ:*

### B. A person's work shall be revealed by fire 1 Cor. 3:13-15 KJV

*13 Every man's work shall be made manifest: for the day shall declare it, because it shall be revealed by fire; and the fire shall try every man's work of what sort it is.*
*14 If any man's work abide which he hath built thereupon, he shall receive a reward.*
*15 If any man's work shall be burned, he shall suffer loss: but he himself shall be saved; yet so as by fire.*

### C. Your fiery trials should not be looked upon as strange but as a part of your walk with Christ 1 Pet. 4:12-14 KJV

*12 Beloved, think it not strange concerning the fiery trial which is to try you, as though some strange thing happened unto you:*
*13 But rejoice, inasmuch as ye are partakers of Christ's sufferings; that, when his glory shall be revealed, ye may be glad also with exceeding joy.*

*14 If ye be reproached for the name of Christ, happy are ye; for the spirit of glory and of God resteth upon you: on their part he is evil spoken of, but on your part he is glorified.*

1. **Fiery** SC NT: ignition, i.e. (specifically) smelting (figuratively, conflagration, calamity as a test)

   a. **Thayers Greek Lexicon**

      1. The burning by which metals are roasted and reduced

      2. By a figure drawn from a refiners fire calamities or trials that test the character

**D. Fire is used to refine metal Zech. 13:9 KJV**

*9 And I will bring the third part through the fire, and will refine them as silver is refined, and will try them as gold is tried: they shall call on my name, and I will hear them: I will say, It is my people: and they shall say, The LORD is my God.*

1. **Refine** SC OT: to fuse (metal), i.e. refine (literally or figuratively)

   **Ps. 66:10** *For thou, O God, hast proved us: thou hast tried us, as silver is tried. KJV*

   **Isa. 48:10** *Behold, I have refined thee, but not with silver; I have chosen thee in the furnace of affliction. KJV*

   **Mal. 3:2-3 KJV**
   *2 But who may abide the day of his coming? and who shall stand when he appeareth? for he is like a refiner's fire, and like fullers' soap:*
   *3 And he shall sit as a refiner and purifier of silver: and he shall purify the sons of Levi, and purge them as gold and silver, that they may offer unto the LORD an offering in righteousness.*

**E. Fire will burn away that which is useless in our lives. Luke 3:16-17 KJV**

*16 John answered, saying unto them all, I indeed baptize you with water; but one mightier than I cometh, the latchet of whose shoes I am not worthy to unloose: he shall baptize you with the Holy Ghost and with fire:*
*17 Whose fan is in his hand, and he will thoroughly purge his floor, and will gather the wheat into his garner; but the chaff he will burn with fire unquenchable.*

1. **Thayers Greek Lexicon Chaff**

   a. A stalk of grain from which the kernels have been beaten out

   b. Straw broken up by a threshing machine, chaff

**F. Fire will remove pollution or dirt from our lives Isa. 4:4 KJV**

*4 When the Lord shall have washed away the filth of the daughters of Zion, and shall have purged the blood of Jerusalem from the midst thereof by the spirit of judgment, and by the spirit of burning.*

1. **Filth** SC OT: excrement; generally, dirt; figuratively, pollution

**G. Fire will try our works to see if they are for real. 1 Cor. 3:13-15 KJV**

*13 Every man's work shall be made manifest: for the day shall declare it, because it shall be revealed by fire; and the fire shall try every man's work of what sort it is.*
*14 If any man's work abide which he hath built thereupon, he shall receive a reward.*
*15 If any man's work shall be burned, he shall suffer loss: but he himself shall be saved; yetso as by fire.*

**H. Fire fulfills the very Word of God Ps. 148:7-8 KJV**

*7 Praise the LORD from the earth, ye dragons, and all deeps:*
*8 Fire, and hail; snow, and vapor; stormy wind fulfilling his word:*

**I. Fire brings light. God led the children of Israel with fire Ex. 13:21 KJV**

*21 And the LORD went before them by day in a pillar of a cloud, to lead them the way; and by night in a pillar of fire, to give them light; to go by day and night:*

a. **John the Baptist was considered a burning light John 5:35 KJV**

*35 He was a burning and a shining light: and ye were willing for a season to rejoice in his light*

1. **Burning** SC NT: to set on fire, i.e. kindle or (by implication) consume

a. **Thayers Greek Lexicon**

1. To set on fire, to light

2. To burn, consume with fire

2. **Light** SC NT: a portable lamp or other illuminators (literally or figuratively)

b. **We are to be burning lights Luke 12:35 KJV**

*35 Let your loins be girded about, and your lights burning;*

**Matt. 5:14** *Ye are the light of the world. A city that is set on an hill cannot be hid.*

1. **Light** SC NT: (to shine or make manifest, especially by rays; luminousness (in the widest application, nat. or artificial, abstract or concrete, literal or figurative)

2. **Thayers Greek Lexicon**

   a. Light

   b. Emitted by a lamp

**Matt. 5:16** *Let your light so shine before men, that they may see your good works, and glorify your Father which is in heaven. KJV*

**V. He uses his fire to bring judgment**

**Ps. 97:3** *A fire goeth before him, and burneth up his enemies round about. KJV*

1. **Sodom and Gomorrah Gen. 19:24-25 KJV**

*24 Then the LORD rained upon Sodom and upon Gomorrah brimstone and fire from the LORD out of heaven;*
*25 And he overthrew those cities, and all the plain, and all the inhabitants of the cities, and that which grew upon the ground.*

2. **Egypt Ex. 9:23-24 KJV**

*23 And Moses stretched forth his rod toward heaven: and the LORD sent thunder and hail, and the fire ran along upon the ground; and the LORD rained hail upon the land of Egypt.*
*24 So there was hail, and fire mingled with the hail, very grievous, such as there was none like it in all the land of Egypt since it became a nation.*

3. **The complaining Israelites were judged with fire Num. 11:1-3 KJV**

*1 And when the people complained, it displeased the LORD: and the LORD heard it; and his anger was kindled; and the fire of the LORD burnt among them, and consumed them that were in the uttermost parts of the camp.*
*2 And the people cried unto Moses; and when Moses prayed unto the LORD, the fire was quenched.*
*3 And he called the name of the place Taberah: because the fire of the LORD burnt among them.*

4. **When Israel captured a city many times they were burnt along with the spoil of the city**

**Deut. 7:25** *The graven images of their gods shall ye burn with fire: thou shalt not desire the silver or gold that is on them, nor take it unto thee, lest thou be snared therein: for it is an abomination to the LORD thy God. KJV*

**Deut. 13:16** *And thou shalt gather all the spoil of it into the midst of the street thereof, and shalt burn with fire the city, and all the spoil thereof every whit, for the LORD thy God: and it shall be an heap for ever; it shall not be built again. KJV*

**Joshua 11:6** *And the LORD said unto Joshua, Be not afraid because of them: for tomorrow about this time will I deliver them up all slain before Israel: thou shalt hough their horses, and burn their chariots with fire. KJV*

## A. Cities burnt with fire

### 1. Jericho Josh. 6:24 KJV

*24 And they burnt the city with fire, and all that was therein: only the silver, and the gold, and the vessels of brass and of iron, they put into the treasury ofthe house of the LORD.*

### 2. Ai Josh. 8:8 KJV

*8 And it shall be, when ye have taken the city, that ye shall set the city on fire: according to the commandment of the LORD shall ye do. See, I have commanded you.*

### 3. Hazor Josh 11:11 KJV

*11 And they smote all the souls that were therein with the edge of the sword, utterly destroying them: there was not any left to breathe: and he burnt Hazor with fire.*

### 4. Cities of Benjamin Judg. 20:48 KJV

*48 And the men of Israel turned again upon the children of Benjamin, and smote them with the edge of the sword, as well the men of every city, as the beast, and all that came to hand: also they set on fire all the cities that they came to.*

# WIND

## INTRO:

**Wind is another symbol that represents the Holy Spirit Acts 2:1-4 KJV**

*1 And when the day of Pentecost was fully come, they were all with one accord in one place.*
*2 And suddenly there came a sound from heaven as of a rushing mighty wind, and it filled all the house where they were sitting.*
*3 And there appeared unto them cloven tongues like as of fire, and it sat upon each of them.*
*4 And they were all filled with the Holy Ghost, and began to speak with other tongues, as the Spirit gave them utterance.*

**I. Man was created to walk and communicate with God. In the garden, God came to man in the cool of the day Gen. 3:1-8 KJV**

*8 And they heard the voice of the LORD God walking in the garden in the cool of the day: and Adam and his wife hid themselves from the presence of the LORD God amongst the trees of the garden.*

1. **Cool** SC OT: wind; by resemblance breath i.e. a sensible (or even violent) exhalation; figuratively, life, anger, by resemblance spirit, but only of a rational being (including its expression and functions)

   a. **SC OT:** to blow, i.e. breathe; only (literally) to smell or (by implication, perceive (figuratively, to anticipate, enjoy)

2. **Brown Driver Briggs Hebrew Dictionary - Wind**

   a. A wind, breath, a mind, a spirit

   b. A wind

      1. Used of heaven

      2. A quarter (used of the wind), aside

      3. A breath of air

4. Air, gas

c. Spirit

1. Spirit, disposition (as troubled, bitter, discontented)

2. Prophetic spirit

3. Spirit (used of the living, breathing being in man and animals); as gift, preserved by God, God's spirit, departing at death, a disembodied being

d. The Spirit of God

1. As an inspiring ecstatic state of prophecy

2. As an impelling prophet to utter instruction or a warning

3. Imparting a war-like energy and executive and administrative power

4. As endowing men with various gifts

5. As an energy of life

**II. There are four winds mentioned in the scripture. Each wind represents a purpose for its existence.**

**A. The east wind**

**1. The east wind represents the destruction of fruitfulness**

a. Pharaoh has a dream which involved an east wind destroying the corn which would cause a famine Gen. 41:5-7 KJV

*5 And he slept and dreamed the second time: and, behold, seven ears of corn came up upon one stalk, rank and good.*
*6 And, behold, seven thin ears and blasted with the east wind sprung up after them.*
*7 And the seven thin ears devoured the seven rank and full ears. And Pharaoh awoke, and, behold, it was a dream.*

**Gen. 41:23-27 KJV**
*23 And, behold, seven ears, withered, thin, and blasted with the east wind, sprung up after them:*
*24 And the thin ears devoured the seven good ears: and I told this unto the magicians; but there was none that could declare it to me.*
*25 And Joseph said unto Pharaoh, The dream of Pharaoh is one: God hath shewed Pharaoh what he is about to do.*
*26 The seven good kine are seven years; and the seven good ears are seven years: the dream is one.*

*27 And the seven thin and ill-favored kine that came up after them are seven years; and the seven empty ears blasted with the east wind shall be seven years of famine.*

1. **Blasted** SC OT: to scorch

b. Ezekiel prophesies about the east wind drying up the fruit Ezek. 19:10-12 KJV

*10 Thy mother is like a vine in thy blood, planted by the waters: she was fruitful and full of branches by reason of many waters.*
*11 And she had strong rods for the sceptres of them that bare rule, and her stature was exalted among the thick branches, and she appeared in her height with the multitude of her branches.*
*12 But she was plucked up in fury, she was cast down to the ground, and the east wind dried up her fruit: her strong rods were broken and withered; the fire consumed them.*

c. Moses stretches his rod over the land of Egypt causing the east wind bring locusts upon the land – a pestilence Ex. 10:13 KJV

*13 And Moses stretched forth his rod over the land of Egypt, and the LORD brought an east wind upon the land all that day, and all that night; and when itwas morning, the east wind brought the locusts.*

2. **The east wind also represents the power of God Ex. 14:21 KJV**

*21 And Moses stretched out his hand over the sea; and the LORD caused the sea to goback by a strong east wind all that night, and made the sea dry land, and the waterswere divided.*

**Ps. 48:7** *Thou breakest the ships of Tarshish with an east wind. KJV*

a. Jonah experienced the east wind - Jonah 4:8 KJV

*8 And it came to pass, when the sun did arise, that God prepared a vehement east wind; and the sun beat upon the head of Jonah, that he fainted, and wished in himself to die, and said, It is better for me to die than to live.*

1. **Vehement** SC OT: silence; quiet, i.e. sultry (hot east wind)

b. Jerimiah prophesies about the east wind Jer. 18:15-17 KJV

*15 Because my people hath forgotten me, they have burned incense to vanity, and they have caused them to stumble in their ways from the ancient paths, to walk in paths, in a way not cast up;*
*16 To make their land desolate, and a perpetual hissing; every one that passeth thereby shall be astonished, and wag his head.*
*17 I will scatter them as with an east wind before the enemy; I will shew them the back, and not the face, in the day of their calamity.*

## B. The west wind

### 1. The west wind speaks of the removal of judgment Ex. 10:13-19 KJV

*13 And Moses stretched forth his rod over the land of Egypt, and the LORD brought an east wind upon the land all that day, and all that night; and when it was morning, the east wind brought the locusts.*
*14 And the locusts went up over all the land of Egypt, and rested in all the coasts of Egypt: very grievous were they; before them there were no such locusts as they, neither after them shall be such.*
*15 For they covered the face of the whole earth, so that the land was darkened; and they did eat every herb of the land, and all the fruit of the trees which the hail had left: and there remained not any green thing in the trees, or in the herbs of the field, through all the land of Egypt.*
*16 Then Pharaoh called for Moses and Aaron in haste; and he said, I have sinned against the LORD your God, and against you.*
*17 Now therefore forgive, I pray thee, my sin only this once, and intreat the LORD your God, that he may take away from me this death only.*
*18 And he went out from Pharaoh, and intreated the LORD.*
*19 And the LORD turned a mighty strong west wind, which took away the locusts, and cast them into the Red sea; there remained not one locust in all the coasts of Egypt.*

a. **West** SC OT: to roar; a sea (as breaking in noisy surf) or large body of water

## C. The north wind

### 1. The north wind speaks to us concerning dark and gloomy – the cold north wind Song 4:16 AMP

*16[You have called me a garden, she said] Oh, I pray that the [cold] north wind and the [soft] south wind may blow upon my garden, that its spices may flow out [in abundance for you in whom my soul delights]. Let my beloved come into his garden and eat its choicest fruits.*

**Prov. 25:23** *The north wind driveth away rain: so doth an angry countenance a backbiting tongue. KJV*

a. **North** SC OT: properly, hidden, i.e. dark; used only of the north as a quarter (gloomy and unknown)

1. **SC OT:** to hide (by covering over); by implication, to hoard or reserve; figuratively to deny; specifically (favorably) to protect, (unfavorably) to lurk

## D. The south wind

### 1. It speaks of the position of authority Ps. 78:26 KJV

*26 He caused an east wind to blow in the heaven: and by his power he brought in the south wind.*

a. **South** SC OT: the south (as being on the right hand of a person facing the east)

1. **SC OT:** the right hand or side (leg, eye) of a person or other object (as the stronger and more dexterous); locally, the south

2. **It speaks of warm weather Luke 12:54-55 KJV**

*54 And he said also to the people, When ye see a cloud rise out of the west, straightway ye say, There cometh a shower; and so it is.*
*55 And when ye see the south wind blow, ye say, There will be heat; and it cometh to pass.*

3. **The south wind is a gentle wind Acts 27:13 KJV**

*13 And when the south wind blew softly, supposing that they had obtained their purpose, loosing thence, they sailed close by Crete.*

**Acts 28:13** *And from thence we fetched a compass, and came to Rhegium: and after one day the south wind blew, and we came the next day to Puteoli: KJV*

**Job 37:17** *How thy garments are warm, when he quieteth the earth by the south wind? KJV*

**Song of Solomon 4:16** *Awake, O north wind; and come, thou south; blow upon my garden, that the spices thereof may flow out. Let my beloved come into his garden, and eat his pleasant fruits. KJV*

III. **Wind - Ezekiel and the dry bones. Ezek. 37:1- 10 KJV**

A. **The word breath is used 4 times in this passage. The word breath means:**

1. **Breath** SC OT: wind; by resemblance breath, i.e. a sensible (or even violent) exhalation; figuratively, life, anger, unsubstantiality; by resemblance spirit, but only of a rational being (including its expression and functions)

*1 The hand of the LORD was upon me, and carried me out in the spirit of the LORD, and set me down in the midst of the valley which was full of bones,*
*2 And caused me to pass by them round about: and, behold, there were very many in the open valley; and, lo, they were very dry.*
*3 And he said unto me, Son of man, can these bones live? And I answered, O Lord GOD, thou knowest.*
*4 Again he said unto me, Prophesy upon these bones, and say unto them, O ye dry bones, hear the word of the LORD.*
*5 Thus saith the Lord GOD unto these bones; Behold, I will cause breath to enter into you, and ye shall live:*
*6 And I will lay sinews upon you, and will bring up flesh upon you, and cover you with skin, and put breath in you, and ye shall live; and ye shall know that I am the LORD.*
*7 So I prophesied as I was commanded: and as I prophesied, there was a noise, and behold a shaking, and the bones came together, bone to his bone.*
*8 And when I beheld, lo, the sinews and the flesh came up upon them, and the skin covered them above: but there was no breath in them.*

*9 Then said he unto me, Prophesy unto the wind, prophesy, son of man, and say to the wind, Thus saith the Lord GOD; Come from the four winds, O breath, and breathe upon these slain, that they may live.*
*10 So I prophesied as he commanded me, and the breath came into them, and they lived, and stood up upon their feet, an exceeding great army.*

**B. It is interesting to note that the breath comes from the four winds. The four winds, each with their different purposes, propel us into the purposes of God.**

1. There are times when the fruit of our lives needs to be challenged

2. There are times when we should be judged, but the mercy of God intervenes

3. There are times for each season of life and fruitfulness. The winter winds blow removing yesterday and setting the stage for spring – new life

4. There are times when we must align ourselves under authority in order to move forward in peace

## IV. The wind comes from God's treasury Ps. 135:7 KJV

*7 He causeth the vapors to ascend from the ends of the earth; he maketh lightnings for the rain; he bringeth the wind out of his treasuries.*

1. **Treasuries** SC OT: a depository:

2. **Brown Driver Briggs Hebrew Dictionary** - a treasure, a storehouse

   a. Treasure (gold, silver, etc.)

   b. Store, supplies of food or drink

   c. Treasure-house, treasury

      1. Treasure-house

      2. Storehouse, magazine

      3. Treasury

      4. Magazine of weapons (figuratively, used of God's armory)

      5. Storehouses (used by God for rain, snow, hail, wind, sea)

**A. The treasuries of heaven contain everything that is needed**

1. **Rain in its proper season Deut. 28:12 KJV**

    *12 The LORD shall open unto thee his good treasure, the heaven to give the rain unto thy land in his season, and to bless all the work of thine hand: and thou shalt lend unto many nations, and thou shalt not borrow.*

2. **Snow and Hail are part of the treasury Job. 38:22 KJV**

    *22 Hast thou entered into the treasures of the snow? or hast thou seen the treasures of the hail,*

3. **The wise have precious treasures and oil Prov. 21:20 AMP**

    *20 There are precious treasures and oil in the dwelling of the wise, but a self-confident and foolish man swallows it up and wastes it.*

4. **He gives treasures of darkness and hidden riches Isa. 45:1-5 KJV**

    *1 Thus saith the LORD to his anointed, to Cyrus, whose right hand I have holden, to subdue nations before him; and I will loose the loins of kings, to open before him the two leaved gates; and the gates shall not be shut;*
    *2 I will go before thee, and make the crooked places straight: I will break in pieces the gates of brass, and cut in sunder the bars of iron:*
    *3 And I will give thee the treasures of darkness, and hidden riches of secret places, that thou mayest know that I, the LORD, which call thee by thy name, am the God of Israel.*
    *4 For Jacob my servant's sake, and Israel mine elect, I have even called thee by thy name: I have surnamed thee, though thou hast not known me.*
    *5 I am the LORD, and there is none else, there is no God beside me: I girded thee, though thou hast not known me:*

5. **The wind is in God's treasures Jer. 51:16 KJV**

    *16 When he uttereth his voice, there is a multitude of waters in the heavens; and he causeth the vapours to ascend from the ends of the earth: he maketh lightnings with rain, and bringeth forth the wind out of his treasures.*

**V. More thoughts about wind**

**A. Life is considered as wind**

1. **Job 7:7** *O remember that my life is wind: mine eye shall no more see good. KJV*

2. **Ps. 78:39** *For he remembered that they were but flesh; a wind that passeth away, and cometh not again. KJV*

3. **James 4:14** *Whereas ye know not what shall be on the morrow. For what is your life? It is even a vapor, that appeareth for a little time, and then vanisheth away. KJV*

    a. **Vapor** SC NT: mist

1. **SCNT:** to breathe unconsciously, i.e. respire; by analogy, to blow); "air" (as naturally circumambient)

**B. The wind can blow away the dark clouds of life Job 37:21 KJV**

*21 And now men see not the bright light which is in the clouds: but the wind passeth, and cleanseth them.*

**C. The ungodly are moved about as chaff before the wind Job 21:17-18 KJV**

*17 How oft is the candle of the wicked put out! and how oft cometh their destruction upon them! God distributeth sorrows in his anger.*
*18 They are as stubble before the wind, and as chaff that the storm carrieth away.*

**Ps. 1:4** *The ungodly are not so: but are like the chaff which the wind driveth away. KJV*

**Ps. 35:5** *Let them be as chaff before the wind: and let the angel of the LORD chase them. KJV*

**Ps. 83:13** *O my God, make them like a wheel; as the stubble before the wind. KJV*

**D. God moves about upon the wind Ps. 104: 1-3 KJV**

*1 Bless the LORD, O my soul. O LORD my God, thou art very great; thou art clothed with honor and majesty.*
*2 Who coverest thyself with light as with a garment: who stretchest out the heavens like a curtain:*
*3 Who layeth the beams of his chambers in the waters: who maketh the clouds his chariot: who walketh upon the wings of the wind:*

**2 Sam. 22:11** *And he rode upon a cherub, and did fly: and he was seen upon the wings of the wind. KJV*

**E. God is the one who causes the wind to blow Ps. 147:18 KJV**

*18 He sendeth out his word, and melteth them: he causeth his wind to blow, and the waters flow.*

**F. God set the wind in circuits around the earth Eccl. 1:6 KJV**

*6 The wind goeth toward the south, and turneth about unto the north; it whirleth about continually, and the wind returneth again according to his circuits.*

**Prov. 30:4** *Who hath ascended up into heaven, or descended? who hath gathered the wind in his fists? who hath bound the waters in a garment? who hath established all the ends of the earth? what is his name, and what is his son's name, if thou canst tell? KJV*

**G. God created the winds Amos 4:13 KJV**

*13 For, lo, he that formeth the mountains, and createth the wind, and declareth unto man what is his thought, that maketh the morning darkness, and treadeth upon the high places of the earth, The LORD, The God of hosts, is his name.*

## VI. Wind is also associated with misleading doctrines Eph. 4:14 KJV

*14 That we henceforth be no more children, tossed to and fro, and carried about with every wind of doctrine, by the sleight of men, and cunning craftiness, whereby they lie in wait to deceive;*

# SEAL

## INTRO:

**Another symbol of the Holy Spirit is a seal. In this lesson we will discover what the seal represents and how it relates to us.**

**I. The seal relates to the Holy Spirit and has a specific purpose. Eph. 1:13 KJV**

*13 In whom ye also trusted, after that ye heard the word of truth, the gospel of your salvation: in whom also after that ye believed, ye were sealed with that Holy Spirit of promise*

1. **Sealed** SC NT: to stamp (with a signet or private mark) for security or preservation (literally or figuratively); by implication, to keep secret, to attest

   a. **Thayers Greek Lexicon**

      1. To set a seal upon, to mark with a seal, to seal
      2. For security: from Satan
      3. Since things sealed up are concealed (as the contents of a letter), to hide, keep in silence, keep secret
      4. In order to mark a person or a thing
         a. To set a mark upon by the impress of a seal or a stamp
         b. Angels are said to be sealed by God
      5. In order to prove, to confirm, or to attest a thing, to confirm authenticate, to place beyond doubt
         a. Used of a written document
         b. To prove one's testimony to a person that he is what he professes to be

2. **SC OT:** a signet (as fencing in or protecting from misappropriation); by implication, the stamp impressed (as a mark of privacy, or genuineness), literally or figuratively:

   a. **Thayers Greek Lexicon**

      1. A seal

      2. The seal placed upon books

      3. A signet ring

      4. The inscription or impression made by a seal; used of the name of God and Christ stamped upon their foreheads

      5. That by which anything is confirmed, proved, authenticated, as by a seal (a token or proof)

3. **SC OT:** to fence or enclose, i.e. (specifically) to block up (figuratively, to silence)

## II. Nelson's Illustrated Bible Dictionary

### A. SEAL

1. A device such as a signet ring or cylinder, engraved with the owner's name, a design, or both Ex. 28:11; Esth. 8:8

2. A medallion or ring used as a seal featured a raised or recessed signature or symbol so it could be impressed on wax or moist clay to leave its mark Job 38:14

3. The seal was strung on a cord and hung around the neck or worn on one's finger Gen. 38:18, RSV; Jer. 22:24

4. A seal usually served to certify a signature or authenticate a letter or other document Neh. 9:38; Esth. 8:8; John 3:33

5. In the New Testament, Pilate authorized a guard to be sent to secure the tomb where the body of Jesus had been laid: "So they went and made the tomb secure, sealing the stone and setting the guard" Matt. 27:66

6. The word seal is used also in a figurative sense of an outward condition John 6:27; 1 Cor. 9:2; 2 Tim. 2:19

7. The Book of Revelation uses the word frequently in this sense Rev. 5:1; 7:2-8; 10:4

## B. SIGNET

1. A seal or ring used by an official much like a personal signature to give authority to a document. The Old Testament indicates several uses of the ring seal

2. Pharaoh gave his ring to Joseph Gen. 41:42 as a badge of his delegated authority

   a. Ahasuerus gave his ring to the wicked Haman Esth. 3:10, 12, then gave it to Mordecai after Haman's treachery was exposed Esth. 8:2

   b. King Darius of Persia sealed the lion's den after Daniel was placed in it Dan. 6:17

3. The signet was an emblem of royal authority Gen. 41:42

   a. Zerubbabel, who had been chosen by God to lead the returned captives in Jerusalem Hag. 2:23, was compared to a signet ring, signifying that God had invested him with the highest honor

## C. JEWELRY

1. Most men wore signet rings for business purposes. These rings were engraved with the owner's name or symbol to show authority or ownership Gen. 38:18; Ex. 28:11; Esth. 8:8; Dan. 6:17

2. The signet rings were worn on the finger or strung around the neck

3. They were usually made of gold and set with an engraved gem

4. Signet rings were given as gifts for the tabernacle Ex. 35:22

**II. We are sealed with the Holy Spirit which is really a down payment on the whole package that God is to bring to pass. II Cor. 1:22 KJV**

*22 Who hath also sealed us, and given the earnest of the Spirit in our hearts.*

1. **Earnest** SC NT: a pledge, i.e. part of the purchase-money or property given in advance as security for the rest

   a. **Thayers Greek Lexicon**

      1. An earnest money which in purchases is given as a pledge or down payment that the full amount will subsequently be paid

**Gen. 38:17-20 KJV**
*17 And he said, I will send thee a kid from the flock. And she said, Wilt thou give me a pledge, till thou send it?*

*18 And he said, What pledge shall I give thee? And she said, Thy signet, and thy bracelets, and thy staff that is in thine hand. And he gave it her, and came in unto her, and she conceived by him.*
*19 And she arose, and went away, and laid by her vail from her, and put on the garments of her widowhood.*
*20 And Judah sent the kid by the hand of his friend the Adullamite, to receive his pledge from the woman's hand: but he found her not.*

2. **Pledge** SC OT: (in the sense of exchange); a pawn (given as security)

    a. **Brown Driver Briggs Hebrew Lexicon**

        1. A pledge, a security

3. **SC OT:** to braid, i.e. intermix; technically, to traffic (as if by barter); also or give to be security (as a kind of exchange)

    a. **Brown Driver Briggs Hebrew Lexicon**

        1. To pledge, to exchange, to mortgage, to engage, to occupy, to undertake for, to give pledges, to be (or to become) surety, to take on a pledge, to give in pledge

**Eph. 4:30** *And grieve not the Holy Spirit of God, whereby ye are sealed unto the day of redemption. KJV*

## III. In the scriptures a seal was used in the following ways

### A. Letters were sealed I Kings 21:8 KJV

*8 So she wrote letters in Ahab's name, and sealed them with his seal, and sent the letters unto the elders and to the nobles that were in his city, dwelling with Naboth.*

1. **Seal** SC OT: a signature-ring

    a. **Brown Driver Briggs Hebrew Lexicon**

        1. A seal, a signet, a signet-ring

2. **SC OT:** to close up; especially to seal

### B. Covenants were sealed Neh. 9:38 KJV

*38 And because of all this we make a sure covenant, and write it; and our princes, Levites, and priests, seal unto it.*

1. **Seal** SC OT: to close up; especially to seal

a. **Brown Driver Briggs Hebrew Lexicon**

1. To seal, to seal up, to affix a seal

C. **Decrees were sealed Esth. 8:8 KJV**

*8 Write ye also for the Jews, as it liketh you, in the king's name, and seal it with the king's ring: for the writing which is written in the king's name, and sealed with the king's ring, may no man reverse.*

**Dan. 6:9** *Wherefore king Darius signed the writing and the decree. KJV*

1. **Decree** SC OT: in a legal sense; an interdict

a. Thayers Greek Lexicon

1. An interdict, a decree, a decree of restriction

2. **SC OT:** an obligation or vow (of abstinence)

3. **SC OT:** to yoke or hitch; by analogy, to fasten in any sense, to join battle

D. **Decrees were signified by a seal I King 21:7-9 KJV**

*7 And Jezebel his wife said unto him, Dost thou now govern the kingdom of Israel? arise, and eat bread, and let thine heart be merry: I will give thee the vineyard of Naboth the Jezreelite.*
*8 So she wrote letters in Ahab's name, and sealed them with his seal, and sent the letters unto the elders and to the nobles that were in his city, dwelling with Naboth.*
*9 And she wrote in the letters, saying, Proclaim a fast, and set Naboth on high among the people:*

**Esth. 8:8-10 KJV**
*8 Write ye also for the Jews, as it liketh you, in the king's name, and seal it with the king's ring: for the writing which is written in the king's name, and sealed with the king's ring, may no man reverse.*
*9 Then were the king's scribes called at that time in the third month, that is, the month Sivan, on the three and twentieth day thereof; and it was written according to all that Mordecai commanded unto the Jews, and to the lieutenants, and the deputies and rulers of the provinces which are from India unto Ethiopia, an hundred twenty and seven provinces, according to their language.*
*10 And he wrote in the king Ahasuerus' name, and sealed it with the king's ring, and sent letters by posts on horseback, and riders on mules, camels, and young dromedaries:*

E. **Deeds of property were sealed Jer. 32:9-14 KJV**

*9 And I bought the field of Hanameel my uncle's son, that was in Anathoth, and weighed him the money, even seventeen shekels of silver.*

*10 And I subscribed the evidence, and sealed it, and took witnesses, and weighed him the money in the balances.*
*11 So I took the evidence of the purchase, both that which was sealed according to the law and custom, and that which was open:*
*12 And I gave the evidence of the purchase unto Baruch the son of Neriah, the son of Maaseiah, in the sight of Hanameel mine uncle's son, and in the presence of the witnesses that subscribed the book of the purchase, before all the Jews that sat in the court of the prison.*
*13 And I charged Baruch before them, saying,*
*14 Thus saith the LORD of hosts, the God of Israel; Take these evidences, this evidence of the purchase, both which is sealed, and this evidence which is open; and put them in an earthen vessel, that they may continue many days.*

**F. Treasures are put in safe places and sealed Deut. 32:34 KJV**

*34 Is not this laid up in store with me, and sealed up among my treasures?*

1. **Treasures** SC OT: a depository

2. **Thayers Greek Lexicon**

   a. A treasure, a storehouse

   b. Treasure (gold, silver, etc.)

   c. Store, supplies of food or drink

   d. Treasure-house, treasury

      1. Treasure-house

      2. Storehouse, magazine

      3. Treasury

      4. Magazine of weapons (figuratively, used of God's armoury)

      5. Storehouses (used by God for rain, snow, hail, wind, sea)

3. **SC OT:** to store up

**Deut. 32:34** *Is not this laid up in store with me, and sealed up among my treasures? KJV*

**G. Daniel was thrown into the prison and the door was sealed Dan. 6:16-17 KJV**

*16 Then the king commanded, and they brought Daniel, and cast him into the den of lions. Now the king spake and said unto Daniel, Thy God whom thou servest continually, he will deliver thee.*
*17 And a stone was brought, and laid upon the mouth of the den; and the king sealed it with his own signet, and with the signet of his lords; that the purpose might not be changed concerning Daniel.*

## H. Jesus' grave was sealed by Pilate Matt. 27:63-66 KJV

*63 Saying, Sir, we remember that that deceiver said, while he was yet alive, After three days I will rise again.*
*64 Command therefore that the sepulchre be made sure until the third day, lest his disciples come by night, and steal him away, and say unto the people, He is risen from the dead: so the last error shall be worse than the first.*
*65 Pilate said unto them, Ye have a watch: go your way, make it as sure as ye can.*
*66 So they went, and made the sepulchre sure, sealing the stone, and setting a watch.*

## I. Circumcision is regarded as a seal of righteousness by faith Rom. 4:11 KJV

*11 And he received the sign of circumcision, a seal of the righteousness of the faith which he had yet being uncircumcised: that he might be the father of all them that believe, though they be not circumcised; that righteousness might be imputed unto them also:*

1. **Seal** SC OT: a signet (as fencing in or protecting from misappropriation); by implication, the stamp impressed (as a mark of privacy, or genuineness), literally or figuratively

2. **Thayers Greek Lexicon**

   a. A seal

   b. The seal placed upon books

   c. A signet ring

   d. The inscription or impression made by a seal; used of the name of God and Christ stamped upon their foreheads

   e. That by which anything is confirmed, proved, authenticated, as by a seal (a token or proof)

## J. God has sealed truth, which can only be opened in his time frames. Dan. 12:8-9 KJV

*8 And I heard, but I understood not: then said I, O my Lord, what shall be the end of these things?*
*9 And he said, Go thy way, Daniel: for the words are closed up and sealed till the time of the end.*

**Rev. 5:1** *And I saw a scroll in the right hand of the one who was sitting on the throne, a scroll with writing on the inside and on the back, and sealed with seven seals.* TLB

# OIL

## INTRO:

**In scripture there are different symbols that represent the Holy Spirit. All of these symbols present a different side of truth concerning the third person of the trinity.**

**A symbol is something that represents something else by association, resemblance, or convention, especially a material object used to represent something invisible.**

**Oil is a symbol of the Holy Spirit 1 Sam. 16:12-13 KJV**

*12 And he sent, and brought him in. Now he was ruddy, and withal of a beautiful countenance, and goodly to look to. And the LORD said, Arise, anoint him: for this is he.*
*13 Then Samuel took the horn of oil, and anointed him in the midst of his brethren: and the Spirit of the LORD came upon David from that day forward. So Samuel rose up, and went to Ramah.*

**Ps. 89:20** *I have found David my servant; with my holy oil have I anointed him: KJV*

**I. Olive Oil was poured upon Priests, Kings, Prophets and Judges in the Old Testament. These were individuals who were called into a serving leadership position**

**A. Priests were anointed Ex. 28:40-41 KJV**

*40 And for Aaron's sons thou shalt make coats, and thou shalt make for them girdles, and bonnets shalt thou make for them, for glory and for beauty.*
*41 And thou shalt put them upon Aaron thy brother, and his sons with him; and shalt anoint them, and consecrate them, and sanctify them, that they may minister unto me in the priest's office.*

**B. Kings were anointed – Saul and David**

**1. Saul was anointed by Samuel 1 Sam. 15:1 KJV**

*1 Samuel also said unto Saul, The LORD sent me to anoint thee to be king over his people, over Israel: now therefore hearken thou unto the voice of the words of the LORD.*

2. **David was anointed by Samuel 1 Sam. 16:11-13 KJV**

*11 And Samuel said unto Jesse, Are here all thy children? And he said, There remaineth yet the youngest, and, behold, he keepeth the sheep. And Samuel said unto Jesse, Send and fetch him: for we will not sit down till he come hither.*

*12 And he sent, and brought him in. Now he was ruddy, and withal of a beautiful countenance, and goodly to look to. And the LORD said, Arise, anoint him: for this is he.*

*13 Then Samuel took the horn of oil, and anointed him in the midst of his brethren: and the Spirit of the LORD came upon David from that day forward. So Samuel rose up, and went to Ramah.*

C. **Prophets were anointed 1 Kings 19:15-16 KJV**

*15 And the LORD said unto Elijah, Go, return on thy way to the wilderness of Damascus: and when thou comest, anoint Hazael to be king over Syria:*

*16 And Jehu the son of Nimshi shalt thou anoint to be king over Israel: and Elisha the son of Shaphat of Abel-meholah shalt thou anoint to be prophet in thy room.*

D. **Judges were anointed**

1. **Othniel the son of Kenaz, Caleb's younger brother Judg. 3:10 KJV**

*10 And the Spirit of the LORD came upon him, and he judged Israel, and went out to war: and the LORD delivered Chushan-rishathaim king of Mesopotamia into his hand; and his hand prevailed against Chushan-rishathaim.*

2. **Gideon Judg. 6:34 KJV**

*34 But the Spirit of the LORD came upon Gideon, and he blew a trumpet; and Abi-ezer was gathered after him.*

a. **Came Upon** SC OT: a primitive root; properly, wrap around, i.e. (by implication) to put on a garment or clothe (oneself, or another), literally or figuratively

3. **Jephthah Judg. 11:29 KJV**

*29 Then the Spirit of the LORD came upon Jephthah, and he passed over Gilead, and Manasseh, and passed over Mizpeh of Gilead, and from Mizpeh of Gilead he passed over unto the children of Ammon.*

4. **Samson Judg. 14:19 KJV**

*19 And the Spirit of the LORD came upon him, and he went down to Ashkelon, and slew thirty men of them, and took their spoil, and gave change of garments unto them which expounded the riddle. And his anger was kindled, and he went up to his father's house.*

E. **All of the people of Israel who were not called to one of these places of responsibility did not have access to the anointing. They had no comprehension of the Holy Spirit coming upon them.**

II. **The 1st mention of anointing was when the people were to bring an offering for the construction of the Tabernacle of Moses Ex. 25:6 KJV**

*6 Oil for the light, spices for anointing oil, and for sweet incense,*

A. **The spices and oil that the people brought for the making of the anointing oil are found in. Ex. 30:22-25 KJV**

*22 Moreover the LORD spake unto Moses, saying,*
*23 Take thou also unto thee principal spices, of pure myrrh five hundred shekels, and of sweet cinnamon half so much, even two hundred and fifty shekels, and of sweet calamus two hundred and fifty shekels,*
*24 And of cassia five hundred shekels, after the shekel of the sanctuary, and of oil olive an hin:*
*25 And thou shalt make it an oil of holy ointment, an ointment compound after the art of the apothecary: it shall be an holy anointing oil.*

1. **Myrrh** SC OT: more (mor); myrrh (as distilling in drops, and also as bitter)

2. **Cinnamon** SC OT: (meaning to erect); cinnamon bark (as in upright rolls)

3. **Calamus/Cane** SC OT: a reed (as erect); by resemblance a rod (especially for measuring), shaft, tube, stem, the radius (of the arm), beam (of a steelyard)

4. **Cassia** SC OT: cassia bark (as in shriveled rolls)

   a. **SC OT:** to shrivel up, i.e. contract or bend the body (or neck) in deference

5. **Olive oil** SC OT: an olive (as yielding illuminating oil), the tree, the branch or the berry

   a. **Hin of Oil** = 5 quarts or six liters

III. **Defining the word anointing in the Old Testament Ex. 29:7 KJV**

*7 Then shalt thou take the anointing oil, and pour it upon his head, and anoint him.*

A. **Anointing** SC OT: unction (the act); by implication, a consecratory gift

1. **Brown Drivers**

   a. Consecrated portion, anointing oil, portion, ointment, anointing portion

**b.** Ointment (used to consecrate by anointing)

**2. American Heritage Dictionary – Consecrate, consecrated, consecrating, consecrates**

**a.** To declare or set apart as sacred

**b.** To initiate (a priest) into the order of bishops

**c.** To dedicate solemnly to a service or goal

**d.** To make venerable; hallow. – consecrate adj. Dedicated to a sacred purpose. Sanctified

**B. SC OT 4886: to rub with oil, i.e. to anoint; by implication, to consecrate; also to paint**

**1. Brown, Driver, Briggs Hebrew Lexicon**

**a.** To smear, to anoint, to spread a liquid

**C. The Priests were anointed resulting in consecration and sanctification for the purpose of ministering Ex. 28:40-41 KJV**

*40 And for Aaron's sons thou shalt make coats, and thou shalt make for them girdles, and bonnets shalt thou make for them, for glory and for beauty.*
*41 And thou shalt put them upon Aaron thy brother, and his sons with him; and shalt anoint them, and consecrate them, and sanctify them, that they may minister unto me in the priest's office.*

**1. Consecrate** SC OT: to set apart as holy, make or declare sacred for religious use, to devote entirely, dedicate

**2. Sanctify** SC OT: to be causatively, make pronounce or observe as clean (ceremonially or morally)

**3. Minister** SC OT: to mediate in religious services, to officiate as a priest, to put on regalia

**IV. In the New Testament Jesus our example is anointed for ministry Luke 4:18-19 KJV**

*18 The Spirit of the Lord is upon me, because he hath anointed me to preach the gospel to the poor; he hath sent me to heal the brokenhearted, to preach deliverance to the captives, and recovering of sight to the blind, to set at liberty them that are bruised,*
*19 To preach the acceptable year of the Lord.*

**1. Anointed** SC NT: through the idea of contact; to smear or rub with oil, i.e. (by implication) to consecrate to an office or religious service:

a. SC NT: to handle); to furnish what is needed; (give an oracle, "graze" [touch slightly], light upon, etc.), i.e. (by implication) to employ or (by extension) to act towards one in a given manner

b. SC NT: (through the idea of hollowness for grasping); the hand (literally or figuratively [power]; especially [by Hebraism] a means or instrument)

c. SC NT: through the idea of a channel), meaning a storm (as pouring rain); by implication, the rainy season, i.e. winter

## A. The New Testament teaches that all individuals can be anointed I John 2:27 KJV

*27 As for you, the anointing you received from him remains in you, and you do not need anyone to teach you. But as his anointing teaches you about all things and as that anointing is real, not counterfeit-just as it has taught you, remain in him.*

1. **Anointing** SC NT: an unguent or smearing, i.e. (figuratively) the special endowment ("chrism") of the Holy Spirit

   a. **Thayers Greek Lexicon**

      1. Anything smeared on, unguent, an ointment, usually prepared by the Hebrews from oil and aromatic herbs

      2. Anointing was the inaugural ceremony for priests

   b. **American Heritage Dictionary**

      1. Inaugurate, inaugurated, inaugurating, inaugurates

2. **SC NT: through the idea of contact; to smear or rub with oil, i.e. (by implication) to consecrate to an office or religious service**

   a. **Thayer's Greek Lexicon**

      1. Consecrating Jesus to the Messianic office, and furnishing him with the necessary powers for its administration

      2. Enduing Christians with the gifts of the Holy Spirit

      3. SC NT: (to handle); to furnish what is needed; (give an oracle, "graze" [touch lightly], light upon, etc.), i.e. (by implication) to employ or (by extension) to act towards one in a given manner

4. SC NT: (through the idea of hollowness for grasping); the hand (literally or figuratively [power]; especially [by Hebraism] a means or instrument)

5. SC NT: (to pour; through the idea of a channel), meaning a storm (as pouring rain); by implication, the rainy season, i.e. winter

**V. What are the purposes for the anointing in our lives? Ex. 30:30-33 KJV**

*30 And thou shalt anoint Aaron and his sons, and consecrate them, that they may minister unto me in the priest's office.*

**A. Anoint and consecrate is to set apart as holy and declare ready for religious work**

1. **Consecrate** SC OT: to be (causatively, make, pronounce or observe as) clean (ceremonially or morally)

**B. To minister is to participate in one's calling**

1. **Minister** SC OT: to mediate in religious services

a. SC OT: literally, one officiating, a priest; also (by courtesy) an acting priest (although a layman)

**C. The anointing is to go from one generation to another. What you have is for the next generation Ex. 30:31 KJV**

*31 And thou shalt speak unto the children of Israel, saying, This shall be an holy anointing oil unto me throughout your generations.*

**Acts 2:38-39 KJV**

*38 Then Peter said unto them, Repent, and be baptized every one of you in the name of Jesus Christ for the remission of sins, and ye shall receive the gift of the Holy Ghost.*

*39 For the promise is unto you, and to your children, and to all that are afar off, even as many as the Lord our God shall call.*

**D. The anointing is not put upon fleshly activity, but spiritual activity Ex. 30:32 KJV**

*32 Upon man's flesh shall it not be poured, neither shall ye make any other like it, after the composition of it: it is holy, and it shall be holy unto you.*

**E. The anointing was not for the purpose of making one feel good, but was for working in your God given responsibilities**

**F. There is no substitute for the real anointing – you have the real thing! Ex. 30:33 KJV**

*33 Whosoever compoundeth any like it, or whosoever putteth any of it upon a stranger, shall even be cut off from his people.*

## G. The anointing is reserved for the people of God – You are blessed Ex. 28:41 KJV

*41 And thou shalt put them upon Aaron thy brother, and his sons with him; and shalt anoint them, and consecrate them, and sanctify them, that they may minister unto me in the priest's office.*

## H. To be anointed was to sanctify or pronounce clean ceremonially or morally

1. **Sanctify** SC OT: to be (causatively, make, pronounce or observe as) clean (ceremonially or morally)

## I. The anointing will enable you to speak boldly Acts 4:29-31 KJV

*29 And now, Lord, behold their threatenings: and grant unto thy servants, that with all boldness they may speak thy word,*
*30 By stretching forth thine hand to heal; and that signs and wonders may be done by the name of thy holy child Jesus.*
*31 And when they had prayed, the place was shaken where they were assembled together; and they were all filled with the Holy Ghost, and they spake the word of God with boldness.*

## J. The anointing enables you to minister to the sick Jam. 5:14 KJV

*14 Is any sick among you? let him call for the elders of the church; and let them pray over him, anointing him with oil in the name of the Lord:*

## K. The anointing enables you to cast out devils Mark 6:13 KJV

*13 And they cast out many devils, and anointed with oil many that were sick, and healed them.*

## L. The anointing will help you fulfill your leadership position

**1 Sam. 2:10** *The adversaries of the LORD shall be broken to pieces; out of heaven shall he thunder upon them: the LORD shall judge the ends of the earth; and he shall give strength unto his king, and exalt the horn of his anointed KJV*

**1 Sam. 2:35** *And I will raise me up a faithful priest, that shall do according to that which is in mine heart and in my mind: and I will build him a sure house; and he shall walk before mine anointed forever. KJV*

**1 Sam. 10:1** *Then Samuel took a vial of oil, and poured it upon his head, and kissed him, and said, Is it not because the LORD hath anointed thee to be captain over his inheritance? KJV*

**1 Sam. 15:17** *And Samuel said, When thou wast little in thine own sight, wast thou not made the head of the tribes of Israel, and the LORD anointed thee king over Israel? KJV*

## M. The anointing will enable God's leaders to defeat their enemies

1. **Othniel Judg. 3:9-10 KJV**

*9 And when the children of Israel cried unto the LORD, the LORD raised up a deliverer to the children of Israel, who delivered them, even Othniel the son of Kenaz, Caleb's younger brother.*
*10 And the Spirit of the LORD came upon him, and he judged Israel, and went out to war: and the LORD delivered Chushan-rishathaim king of Mesopotamia into his hand; and his hand prevailed against Chushan-rishathaim.*

2. **Gideon Judg. 6:34 KJV**

*34 But the Spirit of the LORD came upon Gideon, and he blew a trumpet; and Abiezer was gathered after him.*

3. **Jephthah Judg. 11:29 KJV**

*29 Then the Spirit of the LORD came upon Jephthah, and he passed over Gilead, and Manasseh, and passed over Mizpeh of Gilead, and from Mizpeh of Gilead he passed over unto the children of Ammon.*

4. **David and Goliath 1 Sam. 17:32-37 KJV**

*32 And David said to Saul, Let no man's heart fail because of him; thy servant will go and fight with this Philistine.*
*33 And Saul said to David, Thou art not able to go against this Philistine to fight with him: for thou art but a youth, and he a man of war from his youth.*
*34 And David said unto Saul, Thy servant kept his father's sheep, and there came a lion, and a bear, and took a lamb out of the flock:*
*35 And I went out after him, and smote him, and delivered it out of his mouth: and when he arose against me, I caught him by his beard, and smote him, and slew him.*
*36 Thy servant slew both the lion and the bear: and this uncircumcised Philistine shall be as one of them, seeing he hath defied the armies of the living God.*
*37 David said moreover, The LORD that delivered me out of the paw of the lion, and out of the paw of the bear, he will deliver me out of the hand of this Philistine. And Saul said unto David, Go, and the LORD be with thee.*

## N. The anointing will empower the Believer with gifts 1 Cor. 12:7-11 KJV

*7 But the manifestation of the Spirit is given to every man to profit withal.*
*8 For to one is given by the Spirit the word of wisdom; to another the word of knowledge by the same Spirit;*
*9 To another faith by the same Spirit; to another the gifts of healing by the same Spirit;*
*10 To another the working of miracles; to another prophecy; to another discerning of spirits; to another divers kinds of tongues; to another the interpretation of tongues:*
*11 But all these worketh that one and the selfsame Spirit, dividing to every man severally as he will.*

## VI. Jesus was anointed and ministry flowed from the anointing Luke 4:18 KJV

*18 The Spirit of the Lord is upon me, because he hath anointed me to preach the gospel to the poor; he hath sent me to heal the brokenhearted, to preach deliverance to the captives, and recovering of sight to the blind, to set at liberty them that are bruised,*

**A. The anointing is involved in the preaching of the gospel to the poor**

**B. The anointing is for ministering healing**

**C. The anointing is for preaching deliverance to the captives**

**D. The anointing is for opening blind eyes**

**E. The anointing is for setting at liberty the bruised**

**Acts 10:38** *How God anointed Jesus of Nazareth with the Holy Ghost and with power: who went about doing good, and healing all that were oppressed of the devil; for God was with him. KJV*

**F. The anointing is for doing good**

**G. The anointing is for healing the oppressed**

# BREATH OF GOD

## INTRO:

**The last symbol of the Holy Spirit is the breath of God John 20:21-22 KJV**

*21 Then said Jesus to them again, Peace be unto you: as my Father hath sent me, even so send I you.*
*22 And when he had said this, he breathed on them, and saith unto them, Receive ye the Holy Ghost:*

1. **Breathed** SC NT: (to puff), to blow at or on

   a. **SC NT:** to "puff" or blow, i.e. to swell up; but only used in the implied sense, to germinate or grow (sprout, produce), literally or figuratively

**Gen. 6:17** *And, behold, I, even I, do bring a flood of waters upon the earth, to destroy all flesh, wherein is the breath of life, from under heaven; and everything that is in the earth shall die. KJV*

1. **Breath** SC OT: wind; by resemblance breath, i.e. a sensible (or even violent) exhalation; figuratively, life, anger, unsubstantiality; by extension, a region of the sky; by resemblance spirit, but only of a rational being (including its expression and functions)

   a. **SC OT:** properly, to blow, i.e. breathe; only (literally) to smell or (by implication, perceive (figuratively, to anticipate, enjoy)

**I. The creativity of God is associated with his breath**

**A. The heavens and the host of them were created by his breath Ps. 33:6 KJV**

*6 By the word of the LORD were the heavens made; and all the host of them by the breath of his mouth.*

**Job 26:13** *By his spirit he hath garnished the heavens; his hand hath formed the crooked serpent. KJV*

**B. The creation of the planet earth was by His breath Gen. 1:2 KJV**

*2 And the earth was without form, and void; and darkness was upon the face of the deep. And the Spirit of God moved upon the face of the waters.*

**Ps. 18:15** *Then the channels of waters were seen, and the foundations of the world were discovered at thy rebuke, O LORD, at the blast of the breath of thy nostrils. KJV*

**2 Sam. 22:16** *And the channels of the sea appeared, the foundations of the world were discovered, at the rebuking of the LORD, at the blast of the breath of his nostrils. KJV*

## C. Nature is controlled by the breath of God Job 37:10 KJV

*10 By the breath of God frost is given: and the breadth of the waters is straitened.*

**Ex. 15:8** *And with the blast of thy nostrils the waters were gathered together, the floods stood upright as an heap, and the depths were congealed in the heart of the sea. KJV*

**Gen. 8:1** *And God remembered Noah, and every living thing, and all the cattle that was with him in the ark: and God made a wind to pass over the earth, and the waters asswaged; KJV*

### 1. Locusts were brought and taken away by His breath Ex. 10:13 & 19 KJV

*13 And Moses stretched forth his rod over the land of Egypt, and the LORD brought an east wind upon the land all that day, and all that night; and when it was morning, the east wind brought the locusts.*

*19 And the LORD turned a mighty strong west wind, which took away the locusts, and cast them into the Red sea; there remained not one locust in all the coasts of Egypt.*

### 2. The Red Sea was divided by His breath Ex. 14:21 KJV

*21 And Moses stretched out his hand over the sea; and the LORD caused the sea to go back by a strong east wind all that night, and made the sea dry land, and the waters were divided.*

**Ex. 15:8** *And with the blast of thy nostrils the waters were gathered together, the floods stood upright as an heap, and the depths were congealed in the heart of the sea. KJV*

### 3. The provision of meat (quails) were brought by his breath Num. 11:31 KJV

*31 And there went forth a wind from the LORD, and brought quails from the sea, and let them fall by the camp, as it were a day's journey on this side, and as it were a day's journey on the other side, round about the camp, and as it were two cubits high upon the face of the earth.*

## D. Judgment is issued at the breath of His mouth Isa. 11:4 KJV

*4 But with righteousness shall he judge the poor, and reprove with equity for the meek of the earth: and he shall smite the earth with the rod of his mouth, and with the breath of his lips shall he slay the wicked.*

**Job 4:9** *By the blast of God they perish, and by the breath of his nostrils are they consumed. KJV*

**Isa. 11:4** *But with righteousness shall he judge the poor, and reprove with equity for the meek of the earth: and he shall smite the earth with the rod of his mouth, and with the breath of his lips shall he slay the wicked. KJV*

## II. The breath of God as it relates to mankind

### A. Job declared that the Spirit of God made him and by His breath life was given Job 33:4 KJV

*4 The Spirit of God hath made me, and the breath of the Almighty hath given me life.*

### B. Adam heard the voice of God in the cool of the day. The word cool is the same word as breath Gen. 3:8 KJV

*8 And they heard the voice of the LORD God walking in the garden in the cool of the day: and Adam and his wife hid themselves from the presence of the LORD God amongst the trees of the garden.*

### C. His breath is involved with all of mankind Job 12:10 KJV

*10 In whose hand is the soul of every living thing, and the breath of all mankind.*

**Job 27:3** *All the while my breath is in me, and the spirit of God is in my nostrils; KJV*

### D. The breath of God is involved with the intelligence of man Job 32:8 KJV

*8 But there is a spirit in man: and the inspiration of the Almighty giveth them understanding.*

**Job 32:8** *But there is [a vital force] a spirit [of intelligence] in man, and the breath of the Almighty gives men understanding. [Prov. 2:6.] AMP*

### E. Pharaoh declared that Joseph had the Spirit within him – the breath of God Gen. 41:38 KJV

*38 And Pharaoh said unto his servants, Can we find such a one as this is, a man in whom the Spirit of God is?*

#### 1. Bezaleel a workman appointed to make items of the Tabernacle Ex 31:1-3 KJV

*1 And the LORD spake unto Moses, saying,*
*2 See, I have called by name Bezaleel the son of Uri, the son of Hur, of the tribe of Judah:*
*3 And I have filled him with the spirit of God, in wisdom, and in understanding, and in knowledge, and in all manner of workmanship,*

2. **The seventy elders were given of the same spirit as Moses – the breath of God Num. 11:17-25 KJV**

*17 And I will come down and talk with thee there: and I will take of the spirit which is upon thee, and will put it upon them; and they shall bear the burden of the people with thee, that thou bear it not thyself alone.*

*25 And the LORD came down in a cloud, and spake unto him, and took of the spirit that was upon him, and gave it unto the seventy elders: and it came to pass, that, when the spirit rested upon them, they prophesied, and did not cease.*

## III. The word for breath is also spirit and wind

### A. Spirit

**Prov. 1:23** *Turn you at my reproof: behold, I will pour out my spirit unto you, I will make known my words unto you. KJV*

**Prov. 14:29** *He that is slow to wrath is of great understanding: but he that is hasty of spirit exalteth folly. KJV*

**Prov. 15:4** *A wholesome tongue is a tree of life: but perverseness therein is a breach in the spirit. KJV*

**Prov. 15:13** *A merry heart maketh a cheerful countenance: but by sorrow of the heart the spirit is broken. KJV*

**Prov. 16:19** *Better it is to be of an humble spirit with the lowly, than to divide the spoil with the proud. KJV*

**Prov. 17:27** *He that hath knowledge spareth his words: and a man of understanding is of an excellent spirit. KJV*

**Prov. 18:14** *The spirit of a man will sustain his infirmity; but a wounded spirit who can bear? KJV*

**Prov. 25:28** *He that hath no rule over his own spirit is like a city that is broken down, and without walls. KJV*

**Eccl. 11:5** *As thou knowest not what is the way of the spirit, nor how the bones do grow in the womb of her that is with child: even so thou knowest not the works of God who maketh all. KJV*

**Isa. 11:2** *And the spirit of the LORD shall rest upon him, the spirit of wisdom and understanding, the spirit of counsel and might, the spirit of knowledge and of the fear of the LORD; KJV*

**Isa. 44:3** *For I will pour water upon him that is thirsty, and floods upon the dry ground: I will pour my spirit upon thy seed, and my blessing upon thine offspring: KJV*

## B. Wind

**Ex. 10:13** *And Moses stretched forth his rod over the land of Egypt, and the LORD brought an east wind upon the land all that day, and all that night; and when it was morning, the east wind brought the locusts. KJV*

**Ex. 10:19** *And the LORD turned a mighty strong west wind, which took away the locusts, and cast them into the Red sea; there remained not one locust in all the coasts of Egypt. KJV*

**Ex. 14:21** *And Moses stretched out his hand over the sea; and the LORD caused the sea to go back by a strong east wind all that night, and made the sea dry land, and the waters were divided. KJV*

**Num. 11:31** *And there went forth a wind from the LORD, and brought quails from the sea, and let them fall by the camp, as it were a day's journey on this side, and as it were a day's journey on the other side, round about the camp, and as it were two cubits high upon the face of the earth. KJV*

**2 Sam. 22:11** *And he rode upon a cherub, and did fly: and he was seen upon the wings of the wind. KJV*

**1 Kings 19:11** *And he said, Go forth, and stand upon the mount before the LORD. And, behold, the LORD passed by, and a great and strong wind rent the mountains, and brake in pieces the rocks before the LORD; but the LORD was not in the wind: and after the wind an earthquake; but the LORD was not in the earthquake: KJV*

**Job 21:18** *They are as stubble before the wind, and as chaff that the storm carrieth away. KJV*

**Job 30:22** *Thou liftest me up to the wind; thou causest me to ride upon it, and dissolvest my substance. KJV*

**Job 37:21** *And now men see not the bright light which is in the clouds: but the wind passeth, and cleanseth them. KJV*

**Ps. 1:4** *The ungodly are not so: but are like the chaff which the wind driveth away. KJV*

**Ps. 18:10** *And he rode upon a cherub, and did fly: yea, he did fly upon the wings of the wind. KJV*

**Ps. 83:13** *O my God, make them like a wheel; as the stubble before the wind. KJV*

**Ps. 135:7** *He causeth the vapours to ascend from the ends of the earth; he maketh lightnings for the rain; he bringeth the wind out of his treasuries. KJV*

**Prov. 25:23** *The north wind driveth away rain: so doth an angry countenance a backbiting tongue. KJV*

**Prov. 30:4** *Who hath ascended up into heaven, or descended? who hath gathered the wind in his fists? who hath bound the waters in a garment? who hath established all the ends of the earth? what is his name, and what is his son's name, if thou canst tell? KJV*

**Isa. 41:16** *Thou shalt fan them, and the wind shall carry them away, and the whirlwind shall scatter them: and thou shalt rejoice in the LORD, and shalt glory in the Holy One of Israel. KJV*

**Isa. 57:13** *When thou criest, let thy companies deliver thee; but the wind shall carry them all away; vanity shall take them: but he that putteth his trust in me shall possess the land, and shall inherit my holy mountain; KJV*

**Jer. 10:13** *When he uttereth his voice, there is a multitude of waters in the heavens, and he causeth the vapours to ascend from the ends of the earth; he maketh lightnings with rain, and bringeth forth the wind out of his treasures. KJV*

**Ezek. 37:9** *Then said he unto me, Prophesy unto the wind, prophesy, son of man, and say to the wind, Thus saith the Lord GOD; Come from the four winds, O breath, and breathe upon these slain, that they may live. KJV*

**IV. The breath of God is seen on the day of Pentecost**

**Joel 2:28-29 KJV**

*28 And it shall come to pass afterward, that I will pour out my spirit upon all flesh; and your sons and your daughters shall prophesy, your old men shall dream dreams, your young men shall see visions:*
*29 And also upon the servants and upon the handmaids in those days will I pour out my spirit.*

**Acts 2:1-4 KJV**

*1 And when the day of Pentecost was fully come, they were all with one accord in one place.*
*2 And suddenly there came a sound from heaven as of a rushing mighty wind, and it filled all the house where they were sitting.*
*3 And there appeared unto them cloven tongues like as of fire, and it sat upon each of them.*
*4 And they were all filled with the Holy Ghost, and began to speak with other tongues, as the Spirit gave them utterance.*

**Acts 2:14-16 KJV**

*14 But Peter, standing up with the eleven, lifted up his voice, and said unto them, Ye men of Judaea, and all ye that dwell at Jerusalem, be this known unto you, and hearken to my words:*
*15 For these are not drunken, as ye suppose, seeing it is but the third hour of the day.*
*16 But this is that which was spoken by the prophet Joel;*

**A. The word wind is defined as respiration, a breeze, to breathe hard – the breath of God**

**V. Ezekiel the prophet experienced the Spirit or the breath of God – consider the different ways that the spirit relates: entered, took me up, lifted me up, fell upon me, and carried me out**

**Ezek. 2:1-2 KJV**

*1 And he said unto me, Son of man, stand upon thy feet, and I will speak unto thee.*
*2 And the spirit entered into me when he spake unto me, and set me upon my feet, that I heard him that spake unto me.*

**Ezek. 3:12** *Then the spirit took me up, and I heard behind me a voice of a great rushing, saying, Blessed be the glory of the LORD from his place. KJV*

**Ezek. 3:24** *Then the spirit entered into me, and set me upon my feet, and spake with me, and said unto me, Go, shut thyself within thine house. KJV*

**Ezek. 8:3** *And he put forth the form of an hand, and took me by a lock of mine head; and the spirit lifted me up between the earth and the heaven, and brought me in the visions of God to Jerusalem, to the door of the inner gate that looketh toward the north; where was the seat of the image of jealousy, which provoketh to jealousy. KJV*

**Ezek. 11:1** *Moreover the spirit lifted me up, and brought me unto the east gate of the LORD's house, which looketh eastward: and behold at the door of the gate five and twenty men; among whom I saw Jaazaniah the son of Azur, and Pelatiah the son of Benaiah, the princes of the people. KJV*

**Ezek. 11:5** *And the Spirit of the LORD fell upon me, and said unto me, Speak; Thus saith the LORD; Thus have ye said, O house of Israel: for I know the things that come into your mind, every one of them. KJV*

**Ezek. 11:24** *Afterwards the spirit took me up, and brought me in a vision by the Spirit of God into Chaldea, to them of the captivity. So the vision that I had seen went up from me. KJV*

**Ezek. 37:1** *The hand of the LORD was upon me, and carried me out in the spirit of the LORD, and set me down in the midst of the valley which was full of bones, KJV*

**Ezek. 43:5** *So the spirit took me up, and brought me into the inner court; and, behold, the glory of the LORD filled the house. KJV*

## A. The prophet Ezekiel prophesied and breath came into the slain in Ezek. 37:5-10 KJV

### 1. The prophetic word is also connected to the breath of God.

*5 Thus saith the Lord GOD unto these bones; Behold, I will cause breath to enter into you, and ye shall live:*
*6 And I will lay sinews upon you, and will bring up flesh upon you, and cover you with skin, and put breath in you, and ye shall live; and ye shall know that I am the LORD.*
*7 So I prophesied as I was commanded: and as I prophesied, there was a noise, and behold a shaking, and the bones came together, bone to his bone.*
*8 And when I beheld, lo, the sinews and the flesh came up upon them, and the skin covered them above: but there was no breath in them.*
*9 Then said he unto me, Prophesy unto the wind, prophesy, son of man, and say to the wind, Thus saith the Lord GOD; Come from the four winds, O breath, and breathe upon these slain, that they may live.*
*10 So I prophesied as he commanded me, and the breath came into them, and they lived, and stood up upon their feet, an exceeding great army.*

# BIBLIOGRAPHY


1. Strong, James **Strongs Exhaustive Concordance**
   Nashville, Thomas Nelson Publishers 1984

2. Barnes, Albert **Barnes Notes**
   Baker Books 1983

3. Vine,William Edwy **Vines Expository Dictionary of Biblical Words**
   Old Tappan, New Jersey, Fleming H. Revell Company, 1966

4. American Heritage Publishing Company, **American Heritage Dictionary**
   Boston, Houghton Mifflin 1969

5. Editors Victoria Neufeld and David B. Guralink, **The New World Dictionary, Third College Edition**
   Webster's New World Dictionaries, Cleveland & New York Simon & Schuster, Inc. 1988, 1991

6. Unger, F. Merrill, **Unger's Biblical Dictionary**
   Chicago, Moody Press 1967

7. Ronald F. Youngblood, F.F. Bruce, R.K. Harrison **Nelson's Illustrated Bible Dictionary**
   Thomas Nelson Publishers 1986, 2014

8. Earle, **Adam Clarke's Commentary on the Bible**
   Baker Book House 1987

9. Jamieson, Fausset, and Brown **Commentary on the Whole Bible**
   Grand Rapids, Michigan, Zondervan Publishing House

10. Tenny, Merrill C. Luke **The Wycliffe Bible Commentary**
    Chicago, Moody Press 1962

11. Chad Brand, Eric Mitchell, Holman Reference Editorial Staff
    **Holman Illustrated Bible Dictionary**
    Holman Reference 2015

12. Orr, James (ed.) **International Standard Bible Encyclopedia**
    Grand Rapids: Erdmans 1944

**13.** John McClintock, James Strong, **McClintock and Strong Encyclopedia**
Harper & Brothers, NY 1880

**14.** Thayer, Joseph Henry **Thayers Greek Lexicon**
Grand Rapids, Michigan, Associated Publishers & Authors Inc., 1885

**15.** Francis Brown, Samuel Rolles Driver, Charles Augustus Briggs
**Brown, Driver, Brigg's Hebrew Dictionary** First Published 1906
Hendrickson Publishers

# BIBLES

**TLB** - Scripture quotations marked (TLB) are taken from The Living Bible copyright © 1971.
Used by permission of Tyndale House Publishers, a Division of Tyndale House Ministries, Carol Stream, Illinois 60188. All rights reserved.

**NLT** - Scripture quotations marked (NLT) are taken from the Holy Bible, New Living Translation, copyright ©1996, 2004, 2015 by Tyndale House Foundation.
Used by permission of Tyndale House Publishers, a Division of Tyndale House Ministries, Carol Stream, Illinois 60188. All rights reserved.

**AMP** - "Scripture quotations taken from the Amplified Bible (AMPC),
Copyright 1954, 1958, 1962, 1964, 1965, 1987 by The Lockman Foundation
Used by permission. www.Lockman.org"

**NASB** - "Scripture quotations taken from the New American Standard Bible (NASB)
Copyright 1960, 1962, 1963, 1968, 1971, 1972, 1973, 1975, 1977, 1995
by The Lockman Foundation
Used by permission. www.Lockman.org

**KJV** – King James Version - The King James Version, also known as the King James Bible, sometimes as the English version of 1611, or simply the Authorized Version, is an English translation of the Christian Bible for the Church of England, commissioned in 1604 and completed as well as published in 1611 under the sponsorship of James VI and I. The books of the King James Version include the 39 books of the Old Testament, an intertestamental section containing 14 books of the Apocrypha, and the 27 books of the New Testament. Noted for its "majesty of style", the King James Version has been described as one of the most important books in English culture and a driving force in the shaping of the English-speaking world.

CPSIA information can be obtained
at www.ICGtesting.com
Printed in the USA
BVHW011612130721
611739BV00014B/246